A GATHERING

A GATHERING

A Personal Anthology of Scottish Poems

Edited by
Alexander McCall Smith

with illustrations by
Joe McLaren

Polygon

in association with Carcanet Press Ltd

First published in Great Britain in 2018 by
Polygon, an imprint of Birlinn Ltd,
in association with Carcanet Press Ltd

Birlinn Ltd
West Newington House
10 Newington Road
Edinburgh EH9 1QS

www.polygonbooks.co.uk

9 8 7 6 5 4 3 2 1

ISBN 978 1 84697 404 5

British Library Cataloguing-in-Publication Data
A catalogue record for this book is available on
request from the British Library.

The publisher gratefully acknowledges investment from
Creative Scotland towards the publication of this book.

Typeset in Verdigris MVB by Polygon
Printed and bound by ScandBook, Falun, Sweden

CONTENTS

Poems of Place

Islands

Childhood

Countryside & Animals

Birth, Joy, Life

War, Conflict & Loss

Final Poems & What They Mean to Me

INTRODUCTION

A poem does not have to be famous to be cherished. Most of us are exposed to poetry at school, and we may later take pleasure in remembering some of the poems we learn. But there is another sort of poetic pleasure – that which we get from poems we discover ourselves and commit to our own anthologies. These poems become, for us, a private store of gems – reminders of the very personal nature of poetry, and of the power of a few well-crafted lines to move the reader. Sometimes these poems become something of a talisman to those who know them – lines that will accompany them on their journey through life, remembered at key moments when solace is required, or when they simply want to recall a past moment of insight.

This is a personal collection of poems that I find interesting and enjoyable. My interest in poetry started in childhood, when I was fortunate enough to be exposed to quite a lot of it in one way or another. At school I remember having to learn a certain number of lines of poetry every day and then later recite them. I imagine that this approach to poetry has long since been abandoned, as it must have recruited more enemies of the art form than friends. Yet I do not remember objecting to having to recite long screeds of Longfellow's 'Hiawatha', with its interminable mind-numbing rhythms.

As a student in Edinburgh I started to buy poetry and began to assemble a collection of the works of twentieth-century

Scottish poets. I would look around for copies of titles in the Poetry Scotland series, published in Glasgow by William MacLellan, and for anything by the poets whom I particularly admired at the time – people such as George Bruce, Hugh MacDiarmid, and Sydney Goodsir Smith. Later, when I went to live for a short time in Belfast, I discovered Irish poets, beginning with Michael Longley and the other Ulster poets who were making their mark in the 1970s. That was also the point at which I discovered Auden, beginning a life-long love affair with his remarkable corpus of work.

This anthology has given me the opportunity to think about some of the Scottish poems that have meant something to me. It is not meant to be a representative collection of what Scottish poets have written over the ages – it is purely personal, reflecting no more than my own preferences. Most of the poems included here were written in the twentieth century, and none of them is by a currently living poet. That is not entirely accidental: in any anthology a cut-off point will make the task of selection easier. For this one we decided to only include poets born before the start of the Second World War. I hope that no contemporary poets will take offence at being excluded.

The poems are all Scottish. That is not in any way to undervalue the work of others; it merely stems from my private interest in Scottish literature. Scotland is where I live and it is natural, I think, to love the words that describe your place and the feelings of those who lead their lives there. Scotland is a country that tends to engage people in an especially intense way. Its poetry reflects that – it is full of wistful passion; it is full of longing; it can convey a sense of loss and disappointment; it can be dismissive of pretence and posturing; it can be hard-bitten as much as it can be tender and sentimental; it has little time for artifice. All of that is here in these poems – everything that makes the company of Scottish poets worth cultivating, makes their voices memorable.

Alexander McCall Smith
Edinburgh, 2018

Love & Marriage

Here is a love poem that I discovered quite by chance when I bought a small pamphlet – a mere eighteen pages – published in 1971 by the Castlelaw Press in West Linton. This was a small press that published beautiful limited editions from a Peebleshire village. I had never heard of the poet, Kate Y.A. Bone, who was born in 1897 and died in 1986. She was by no means famous; I have not been able to speak to anybody who knew her, and I know next to nothing about her life. But she wrote some memorable poems, including this one, taken from *Thistle By-Blaws*, that small pamphlet I came across in a second-hand book shop.

Some Ghaists Haunt Hooses

Some ghaists haunt hooses, this ane haunts my hert,
An' aye I harken for its lichtlie step
That gars a stound gan thru'me. Ilka pairt   *ache; each*
Is rugged tae mind what aince this meant tae me.
Nae skeleton I see; this ghaist is busked in flesh,
An' a' my thochts are hidden in the bluid   *thoughts; blood*
That feels the dule, but disna bode tae tell
What aince I felt but noo I maun forbear.
Some ghaists haunt hooses, this ane haunts my hert.

KATE Y.A. BONE

The idea that we may have a ghost in our heart is a striking one. The heart has a troubled time in literature: it may be broken, rent, split in two; it may beat fiercely with emotion and longing; it may move us to act against the promptings of another part of the body – the head; it may falter and become still. The heart, then, has a great deal of metaphorical work to do.

The repeated line 'Some ghaists haunt hooses, this ane haunts my hert' will surely resonate with anybody who has loved somebody and then has lost that love for one reason or another. It will resonate, too, with anybody who has experienced unrequited or undeclared love. Years later, the ghost of that love may still linger in memory, lodged somewhere in the chambers of the heart.

Love defies explanation. Love is like electricity – something we know is there but cannot see. Love touches us all with its healing hand, may wipe away our tears, may make us whole again, may restore to us that which we have lost and thought we never would regain. A poem about love may make us feel that the world, for a brief moment, is once again as we would like it to be.

Of the poems in this section, three stand out for me. Edwin Morgan's 'Strawberries' captures that heightened sense of moment and place that accompanies the experience of love. We tend to remember where we were at such times: the party where the meeting happened, the music we were listening to, the way the sky looked. The encounter he describes took place to the accompaniment of strawberries, with lightning on the Kilpatrick hills. Two things, strawberries and lightning, become memorable and special because they form the backdrop to passion. The other love poem of Morgan's that is included here is beautiful in a similarly physically intense way, but is marred for me by the tobacco imagery. A lover with tobacco lips may have been romantic in the past but that, alas, dates the poem. A lover with tobacco lips would find it increasingly difficult to get anybody to kiss them today. Or perhaps that's just wishful thinking on my part.

Then there is Robert Burns' incomparable 'A Red, Red Rose'. No selection of Scottish love poetry would be complete without this dearly loved poem, often sung, of course. This has the majesty of perfection: there is no word here that is otiose, or out of place, or jarring in any way. And what noble determination is there in those heart-rending lines: 'And I will luve thee still, my Dear, / Till a' the seas gang dry. / Till a' the seas gang dry, my Dear, / And the rocks melt wi' the sun'! For most people, of course, when they are in love it is inconceivable that they will fall out of it, and it is sometimes a surprise when that occurs. On the first such occasion, the thought may come to mind: how is it possible that this can happen?

Undeclared love is a poignant theme for the novelist, as it is for the poet. Some go through their lives loving one to whom they can never profess their love, for whatever reason – some private feeling of shame, some conspiracy of circumstance, some cruel climate of disapproval. Or even timidity, and the tying of the tongue that goes with timidity. 'Watching You Walk' by Ruthven Todd has the poet lying with his love as she reads him Wilfred Owen: 'and I, too deeply moved / Watched the swans for a moment, before I spoke / The trivialities, unable to tell you how I loved.' Most of us can remember times when we did not say something we should have said, and then found out it was too late. Poetry is sometimes the way in which people express things the heart wants to say but for which no spoken words can be found.

True ways of knowing

Not an ounce excessive, not an inch too little,
Our easy reciprocations. You let me know
The way a boat would feel, if it could feel,
The intimate support of water.

The news you bring me has been news forever,
So that I understand what a stone would say
If only a stone could speak. Is it sad a grassblade
Can't know how it is lovely?

Is it sad that you can't know, except by hearsay
(My gossiping failing words) that you are the way
A water is that can clench its palm and crumple
A boat's confiding timbers?

But that's excessive, and too little. Knowing
The way a circle would describe its roundness,
We touch two selves and feel, complete and gentle,
The intimate support of being.

The way that flight would feel a bird flying
(If it could feel) is the way a space that's in
A stone that's in water would know itself
If it had our way of knowing.

NORMAN MacCAIG

Incident

I look across the table and think
(fiery with love)
Ask me, go on, ask me
to do something impossible,
something freakishly useless,
something unimaginable and inimitable
like making a finger break into blossom
or walking for half an hour in twenty minutes
or remembering tomorrow.

I will you to ask it.
But all you say is
Will you give me a cigarette, please?
And I smile and,
returning to the marvellous world
of possibility,
I give you one
with a hand that trembles
with a human trembling.

NORMAN MacAIG

To a Lady

Sweet rois of vertew and of gentilness,
Delytsum lily of everie lustynes,
  Richest in bontie and in bewtie clear,
  And everie vertew that is wenit dear,
Except onlie that ye are mercyless,

Into your garth this day I did persew;
There saw I flowris that fresche were of hew;
  Baith quhyte and reid most lusty were to seyne,
  And halesome herbis upon stalkis greene;
Yet leaf nor flowr find could I nane of rew.

I doubt that Merche, with his cauld blastis keyne,
Has slain this gentil herb, that I of mene;
  Quhois piteous death dois to my heart sic paine
  That I would make to plant his root againe,
So confortand his levis unto me bene.

WILLIAM DUNBAR

[8]

Mary's Song

I wad ha'e gi'en him my lips tae kiss,
Had I been his, had I been his;
Barley breid and elder wine,
Had I been his as he is mine.

The wanderin' bee it seeks the rose;
Tae the lochan's bosom the burnie goes;
The grey bird cries at evenin's fa',
'My luve, my fair one, come awa'.'

My beloved sall ha'e this he'rt tae break,
Reid, reid wine and the barley cake;
A he'rt tae break, and a mou' tae kiss,
Tho' he be nae mine, as I am his.

MARION ANGUS

One Cigarette

No smoke without you, my fire.
After you left,
your cigarette glowed on in my ashtray
and sent up a long thread of such quiet grey
I smiled to wonder who would believe its signal
of so much love. One cigarette
in the non-smoker's tray.
As the last spire
trembles up, a sudden draught
blows it winding into my face.
Is it smell, is it taste?
You are here again, and I am drunk on your tobacco lips.
Out with the light.
Let the smoke lie back in the dark.
Till I hear the very ash
sigh down among the flowers of brass
I'll breathe, and long past midnight, your last kiss.

EDWIN MORGAN

Strawberries

There were never strawberries
like the ones we had
that sultry afternoon
sitting on the step
of the open french window
facing each other
your knees held in mine
the blue plates in our laps
the strawberries glistening
in the hot sunlight
we dipped them in sugar
looking at each other
not hurrying the feast
for one to come
the empty plates
laid on the stone together
with the two forks crossed
and I bent towards you
sweet in that air
in my arms
abandoned like a child
from your eager mouth
the taste of strawberries
in my memory

lean back again
let me love you

let the sun beat
on our forgetfulness
one hour of all
the heat intense
and summer lightning
on the Kilpatrick hills

let the storm wash the plates

EDWIN MORGAN

The Shadows

'I think,' she said, 'we shall not see again
each other as we did.' The light is fading
that was once sunny in the April rain.
Across the picture there appears a shading
we didn't notice, but was in the grain.

The picture shows two people happily smiling
with their arms around each other, by the sea.
Whatever they are looking at is beguiling
themselves to themselves. There is a tree
with orange blossoms and an elegant styling

but they are lost quite clearly in each other.
They do not see the landscape, do not hear
the stream that tinkles through the azure weather.
It's as if really the clear atmosphere
were a creation of two souls together.

But at the back there steadily grow two shadows
one for each lover that they can't evade.
They emerge threateningly from the coloured meadows
as if they were a track the two had made
and they were ignorant of, their changeless natures.

And as they move the shades intently follow
growing steadily darker, spreading as they go
as the wings' shades pursue the flying swallow.

My dearest love, if these should make us slow –
remember last the first undying halo.

IAIN CRICHTON SMITH

A Red, Red Rose

O my Luve is like a red, red rose
  That's newly sprung in June;
O my Luve is like the melody
  That's sweetly played in tune.

So fair art thou, my bonnie lass,
  So deep in luve am I;
And I will luve thee still, my Dear,
  Till a' the seas gang dry.

Till a' the seas gang dry, my Dear,
  And the rocks melt wi' the sun;
I will luve thee still, my dear,
  While the sands o' life shall run.

And fare thee weel, my only Luve!
  And fare thee weel, a while!
And I will come again, my Luve,
  Tho' it were ten thousand mile.

ROBERT BURNS

Tràighean

Nan robh sinn an Talasgar air an tràigh
far a bheil am beul mòr bàn
a' fosgladh eadar dà ghiall chruaidh,
Rubha nan Clach 's am Bioda Ruadh,
sheasainn-sa ri taobhn na mara
ag ùrachadh gaoil 'nam anam
fhad 's a bhiodh an cuan a'lìonadh
camas Thalasgair gu sìorraidh:
sheasainn an siud air lom na tràghad
gu 'n cromadh Priseal a cheann àigich.

Agus nan robh sinn ciudeachd
air tràigh Chalgaraidh am Muile,
eadar Alba is Tiriodh,
eadar an saoghal 's a' bhiothbhuan,
dh'fhuirichinn an siud gu luan
a' tomhas gainmhich bruan air bhruan.
Agus an Uibhist air tràigh Hòmhstadh
fa chomhair farsaingeachd na h-ònrachd,
dh'fheithinn-sa an siud gu sìorraidh
braon air bhraon an cuan a' sìoladh.

Agus nan robh mi air tràigh Mhùideart
còmhla riut, a nodhachd ùidhe,
chuirinn suas an co-chur gaoil dhut
an cuan 's a' ghaineamh, bruan air bhraon dhiubh.
'S nan robh sinn air Mol Steinnseil Stamhain

Shores

If we were in Talisker on the shore
where the great white mouth
opens between two hard jaws,
Rubha nan Clach and the Bioda Ruadh,
I would stand beside the sea
renewing love in my spirit
while the ocean was filling
Talisker bay forever:
I would stand there on the bareness of the shore
until Prishal bowed his stallion head.

And if we were together
on Calgary shore in Mull,
between Scotland and Tiree,
between the world and eternity,
I would stay there till doom
measuring sand, grain by grain,
and in Uist, on the shore of Homhsta
in presence of that wide solitude,
I would wait there forever
for the sea draining drop by drop.

And if I were on the shore of Moidart
with you, for whom my care is new,
I would put up in a synthesis of love for you
the ocean and the sand, drop and grain.
And if we were on Mol Stenscholl Staffin

's an fhairge neo-aoibhneach a' tarraing
nan ulbhag is gan tilgeil tharainn,
thogainn-sa am balla daingeann
ro shìorraidheachd choimhich 's i framhach.

SOMHAIRLE MacGILL-EAIN

when the unhappy surging sea dragged
the boulders and threw them over us,
I would build the rampart wall
against an alien eternity grinding (its teeth).

SORLEY MacLEAN

Watching You Walk

Watching you walk slowly across a stage,
Suddenly I am become aware of all the past;
Of all the tragic maids and queens of every age,
Of Joan, whose love the flames could not arrest.

Of those to whom always love was the first duty,
Who saw behind the crooked world the ugly and weak,
Whose kindliness was no gesture; no condescending pity
Could rule their actions; those whom Time broke,

But whom he could not totally destroy.
Hearing the truth you give to these dead words,
Whose writer feared the life they might enjoy,
I can recall the mating orchestra of birds

Behind your voice, as lying by the lake,
You read me Owen, and I, too deeply moved,
Watched the swans for a moment, before I spoke
The trivialities, unable to tell you how I loved.

Watching your fingers curl about a painted death,
I am suddenly glad that it is April, that you are queen
Of all the sordid marches of my bruised heart,
That, loving you, the poplars never seemed so green;

Glad of my lonely walk beside the shrunken river,
Thinking of you while seeing the tufts of ash,
The chestnut candles and unreal magnolia's wax flower;
Glad that, in loving you, the whole world lives afresh.

RUTHVEN TODD

'I will make you brooches and toys for your delight'

I will make you brooches and toys for your delight
Of bird-song at morning and star-shine at night.
I will make a palace fit for you and me
Of green days in forests and blue days at sea.

I will make my kitchen, and you shall keep your room,
Where white flows the river and bright blows the broom,
And you shall wash your linen and keep your body white
In rainfall at morning and dewfall at night.

And this shall be for music when no one else is near,
The fine song for singing, the rare song to hear!
That only I remember, that only you admire,
Of the broad road that stretches and the roadside fire.

ROBERT LOUIS STEVENSON

Sonnet

My love grows, and yet mair on mair shall grow
As lang as I hae life: O happy pairt,
Alane tae haud a place in that dear hairt
Tae which in time my love itsel shall show
Sae clear that he can nane misdoot me then!
For him I will staun stieve agin sair fate,
For him I will strive for the heichest state,
And dae sae muckle for him he shall ken
I naethin hae – nae gowd, nae gear, nae pleisure –
But tae obey and serve him in haill meisure.
For him I hope for aw guid chance and graith;
For him I will me keep baith quick and weel;
True smeddum I desire for him and feel,
And never will I change while I hae braith.

MARY QUEEN OF SCOTS
'Mon amour croist, et plus en
plus croistra'
translated from French by
JAMES ROBERTSON

Poems of Place

Poetry often expresses feeling for place and the intensity of the reaction the poet has to a landscape in all its moods. Poetry may take place nowhere in particular – other than in a realm of ideas – but much poetry is evocative not only of a particular moment but also of the place where that moment happens. Poetry may be like an impressionist painter: dabbing small images on the canvas of our imagination until suddenly there is a composite whole before us – a delicately painted world.

Place may also be the inspiration, the trigger of the poetic impulse. Poets commit to poetry because they wish somehow to capture the essence of a particular place. Auden said of Yeats that Ireland *hurt* him into poetry. Scotland does that too, as Hugh MacDiarmid so memorably wrote in his poem, 'The Little White Rose':

> The rose of all the world is not for me.
> I want for my part
> Only the little white rose of Scotland
> That smells sharp and sweet – and breaks the heart.

In MacDiarmid's view there are other flowers, too, that express Scotland. In "Scotland small?" the poet recites a botanical checklist of reasons why Scotland is *not* small.

'Scotland small?'

Scotland small? Our multiform, our infinite Scotland *small*?
Only as a patch of hillside may be a cliché corner
To a fool who cries 'Nothing but heather!' where in September another
Sitting there and resting and gazing around
Sees not only the heather but blaeberries
With bright green leaves and leaves already turned scarlet
Hiding ripe blue berries; and amongst the sage-green leaves
Of the bog-myrtle the golden flowers of the tormentil shining;
And on the small bare places, where the little Blackface sheep
Found grazing, milkworts blue as summer skies;
And down in neglected peat-hags, not worked
Within living memory, sphagnum moss in pastel shades
Of yellow, green, and pink; sundew and butterwort
Waiting with wide-open sticky leaves for their tiny winged prey;
And nodding harebells vying in their colour
With the blue butterflies that poise themselves delicately upon them;
And stunted rowans with harsh dry leaves of glorious colour.
'Nothing but heather!' – How marvellously descriptive! And incomplete!

HUGH MacDIARMID

[28]

And here are two more poems simply about Scotland. Not every poem is unbridled in its admiration for the country or its people. In the first of these poems, Alistair Reid, a cosmopolitan Scot who lived much of his life overseas, pokes fun at the dour Calvinist streak in the national character. There are other streaks, of course – many of them positive – but we will all recognise this one.

Scotland

It was a day peculiar to this piece of the planet,
when larks rose on long thin strings of singing
and the air shifted with the shimmer of actual angels.
Greenness entered the body. The grasses
shivered with presences, and sunlight
stayed like a halo on hair and heather and hills.
Walking into town, I saw, in a radiant raincoat,
the woman from the fish-shop. 'What a day it is!'
cried I, like a sunstruck madman.
And what did she have to say for it?
Her brow grew bleak, her ancestors raged in their graves
as she spoke with their ancient misery:
'We'll pay for it, we'll pay for it, we'll pay for it!'

ALASTAIR REID

Scotland

Here in the Uplands
The soil is ungrateful;
The fields, red with sorrel,
Are stony and bare.
A few trees, wind-twisted –
Or are they but bushes?
Stand stubbornly guarding
A home here and there.

Scooped out like a saucer,
The land lies before me;
The waters, once scattered,
Flow orderly now
Through fields where the ghosts
Of the marsh and the moorland
Still ride the old marches,
Despising the plough.

The marsh and the moorland
Are not to be banished;
The bracken and heather,
The glory of broom,
Usurp all the balks
And the fields' broken fringes,
And claim from the sower
Their portion of room.

This is my country,
The land that begat me.
These windy spaces
Are surely my own.
And those who here toil
In the sweat of their faces
Are flesh of my flesh,
And bone of my bone.

Hard is the day's task –
Scotland, stern Mother –
Wherewith at all times
Thy sons have been faced –
Labour by day,
And scant rest in the gloaming,
With want an attendant,
Not lightly outpaced.

Yet do thy children
Honour and love thee.
Harsh is thy schooling,
Yet great is the gain:
True hearts and strong limbs,
The beauty of faces,
Kissed by the wind
And caressed by the rain.

SIR ALEXANDER GRAY

Ruthven Todd had an unusual career for a Scottish poet. Born in Edinburgh in 1914, he was educated at Fettes College and the Edinburgh College of Art. The latter (now part of the University of Edinburgh) claims him as one its distinguished graduates, but it is not as an artist that Todd was to make his name but as a writer. His poetry was never as well known as his other writings – particularly his work on William Blake – but wider recognition of its worth is long overdue.

Todd moved to London, where he involved himself with literary circles. He knew Dylan Thomas, Geoffrey Grigson and Julian Symons. In 1947 he went to live in the United States, where he wrote a number of children's books. He moved to Spain in 1960 and died in a mountain village there in 1978. His poems are now scattered among out-of-print collections and the occasional anthology; he is not widely remembered, but those who appreciate his work discern in it an exceptional beauty and poignancy. He has a gift for creating a sense of place and for heightening our feeling for the historical moment.

Todd's poem 'In Edinburgh 1940' embraces the sweep of the city's history, while maintaining, as this poem demonstrates, the personal voice that the poet handles so effectively – and so lightly.

In Edinburgh 1940

I

Now, O let lovers lie close near Cramond Brig
And the children gather the frail clams beside Hound Point,
Beside the little island with wooden beacon.
O let the summer ripen the clustered rowans,
And the fronds of bracken curl over the Pentland Hills.
Though the May Island be blinded by war, let the fish
Run through the booms, and the Forth break to the sea.

Under the lion-crouching shadow of Arthur's Seat,
Let me walk by the ruined palace, in the vision of history.
Let me walk by the volcanic rock, basalt crowned with the Castle,
In Charlotte Square let me hear Sir Walter Scott droning,
Drivelling a dream of history, and let me meet Burns,
Outside the Tron Bar, drunk with disgust as much as whisky:

In time of war let me ask him the expected questions –
Ask whether his rocks have melted with the sun
This summer, and whether the tides have all gone dry
Along the Ayrshire coast. O let me observe his distaste
For my cigarettes and half-pint of beer, my snigger of sex.
O do not leave me alone with the ghosts of the past.

II

I was born in this city of grey stone and bitter wind,
Of tenements sooted up with lying history:
This place where dry minds grow crusts of hate, as rocks
Grow lichens. I went to school over the high bridge

Fringed with spikes which, curiously, repel the suicides;
And I slept opposite the rock-garden where the survivors,
Who had left Irving and Mallory under the sheet of snow,
Planted the incarvillea and saxifrages of the Himalayas.

And, as I grew in childhood, I learned the knack to slip
The breech-block of the field-gun in the park, peering
Along the rifled barrel I would enclose a small circle
Of my world, marked out for death; death as unreal
At the gun's forgotten action under the hot African sun.
Growing older, I met other and more frequent ghosts,
Lying to preserve the remnants of a reputation.

Knox spoke sweetly in the Canongate – 'I was not cruel
To gaunt Mary, the whore denying the hand that lit the fuse.'
Charles Stuart returned, alive only to the past, his venture
That was little but a dream, forgetting the squat bottle,
Quivered in the lace-veined hand and the unseeing sharpness of
    his eyes.
Bruce could not stir the cobwebs from his skeleton,
And the editor spoke regretfully, but firmly, of poor Keats.

Here the boy Rimbaud paused, flying love and lust,
Unnoticed on his journey to the Abyssinian plains
And the thick dropsy of his tender leg. Here the other Knox,
Surgeon and anatomist, saw the beauty of the young girl
Smothered by Burke and Hare. And here, O certainly,
God was the private property of a chosen few
Whose lives ran carefully and correctly to the grave.

This, deny it as I like, is still my city and these ghosts,
Sneer as I may, have helped to make me what I am.
A woman cried in labour and Simpson inhaled his vapour
Falling, anaesthetised, across the drawing-room table.
John Graham, laird of Claverhouse, did not have tears
For those he killed, nor did the silver bullet weep for him.
This city, bulwark of the east wind, formed me as I am.

III

I am the Crusoe of my heart, lord of the vague nerve,
John seeing the sixth seal opened and the curtain of blood
Shuttering my mind, Simon, perched on the twin columns
Of my legs, St. Lawrence roasted on the gridiron of my skeleton.
I am Christ crucified upon the cross-bow of my ribs.

I was the boy following Childe Harold up the Rhine,
Who saw Cortez conquer Mexico and the golden sun
Overthrown, who slept beside the Martello tower
To watch the beacons flare, from Kent to Cumberland;
Who saw Richthofen, dead, land safely on the earth.

O I was these in dreams, and in my shadow I detect
Their shapes. Their hands grapple and fingers point
From the trees in the public parks, and they accuse
Me always. They are the masters of my failure
And can cover me with the green darkness of their night.

'Remember,' the universal voice speaks, 'the Flaming Mountain,
My River of Ice that would not cool my Burns,

The Revelation on Patmos and the Footprint in the Sand,
Remember, O can you forget? Napoleon: that Winter
Of Snow and Fire; the Rocking Horse on the Island.

Remember Trelawny removing the specially fashioned Boot,
To find as he desired, the Cloven Hoof, and that small Hill
Shaped like a Skull, and the dead Hands on the Pilot's Stick.
O recall these Things, for they, also, were a Part;
They were the Milky Way of Dreams, Hoops to your Mind's Staves.'

IV

Now I ask love from the stars in a time of hate
And, also, beg peace from the voice of the dead.
I cannot, however much I desire it, deny the past.
What, I say to the midsummer moon, can I do in this city,
And where can I walk to avoid the lies of history?

From my place here, beside the cemetery where the poisoner
Hid his evidence, I walk among the cities of the weeping world;
Stumble among the ruins of Madrid and lean on the framework
That once was Warsaw, look at Oslo and Copenhagen,
And at the latest city, Paris, where dreams where tough as steel.

O in this bright summer of a breaking world
I write these lines as a memorial to this city,
This outpost, one of many, of my ingenuous heart,
Remembering its history as a pile of trash
And its teaching false as the light of a dead star.

O the green walnut of my heart is hard and dry
On this occasion devoted to the repertory of death:
I remark that the lying legend of this town
Makes no concession to those who are alive.
This city, truant of time, is lost, alas, in history.

RUTHVEN TODD

Ruthven Todd was a product of bourgeois Edinburgh; Robert Sutherland, who wrote as Robert Garioch, came from a very different background. His father was a porter in Leith, accustomed to the back-breaking work of carrying heavy sacks of grain from ship to shore, but, like many a Scottish father before him, he was determined to give his son the best education he could possibly afford. Garioch's achievement, both as a poet writing in the Scots tradition and as a translator of Italian poetry, was considerable. There was a certain fashion for regarding him as simply a witty satirist; he was far more than that. And yet, his satire contains egregious gems, particularly when he is writing about Edinburgh, a city of famous contrasts between respectability and its less salubrious underbelly.

A familiar figure in this uneasy co-existence of the genteel and the rough is the pompous councillor, promoted above himself and very conscious of his dignity. Garioch understood such people well, and in 'Did You See Me?' portrays with perfect pitch such a self-important municipal figure. The theme of the poem is simple: there is a grand civic occasion, and our narrator is delighted to be invited. Unfortunately, the 'keelies of the toun', the town ruffians, get to hear of the event and turn up to spoil it. This is a delightful picture; we can just see them, laughing, yes laughing, at the gathered worthies – one of whom, the narrator, has a particular reason to feel embarrassed by the whole affair. The result is one of the most amusing poems ever written in Scots. This poem is a glorious joke to all those who understand Edinburgh's pretensions.

Did You See Me?

I'll tell ye of ane great occasioun:
I tuke pairt in a graund receptioun.
Ye cannae hae the least perceptioun
How pleased I was to get the invitatioun

tae assist at ane dedicatioun.
And richtlie sae; frae its inceptioun
The hale ploy was my ain conceptioun;
I was asked to gie a dissertatioun.

The function was held in the aipen air,
a peety, that: the keelies of the toun,
a toozie lot, gat word of the affair.

We cudnae stop it: they jist gaitherrt roun
to mak sarcastic cracks and grin and stare.
I wisht I hadnae worn my M.A. goun.

ROBERT GARIOCH

Poor man; to get dressed up in one's M.A. gown and then to be laughed at by in public must be intensely humiliating. But richly funny. These unhelpful 'keelies' were described by Garioch as 'toozie'. Toozie, which is also spelt as tousy, means in Scots unkempt or ragged. It usually refers to hair, but may be used in relation to clothing or, indeed, to an overall scruffy appearance. A high wind may make even cattle look tousy, as the *Scots Magazine* reports in 1925: 'On whinny braes the towzie kye bide dourly till the storm blaws by'. And the *Dictionary of the Scots Language* lists the increasingly wide meaning of the word, to describe rough weather and, curiously, a 'tea with all the trimmings'.

Garioch wrote a poem about one of Edinburgh's landmarks, Princes Street Gardens, which runs adjacent to Princes Street, a subject also visited by Norman MacCaig. These two follow shortly.

And here is another of Garioch's tilts at Edinburgh pomp, 'Glisk of the Great'. In this case, the narrator cannot join in the spectacle of civic grandeur, but likes the 'tone' it imparts to the town. As with much of Garioch's Scots poetry, it is barely necessary to know the precise meaning of all the Scots words; his language is so anchored in the everyday usage with which he was brought up, that it is easy, I suspect, for anybody – even those unaccustomed to Scots – to know exactly what is going on. 'Glisk' here means glimpse. The N.B. Grill is the grand grill of what used to be the North British Hotel or the N.B. – a name still used by diehard opponents of the renaming of great old hotels just because they have been acquired by a chain or because the names fondly given them by the locals are thought to be insufficiently grand. So, while there are some who may call the hotel by its current name, The Balmoral, for others it will always be the N.B. Hotel.

Glisk of the Great

I saw him comin out the N.B. Grill,
creashy and winey, wi his famous voice
crackin some comic bawr to please three choice
notorious bailies, lauchan fit to kill.

Syne thae fowre crousie cronies clam intill
a muckle big municipal Rolls-Royce,
and disappeared, aye lauchan, wi a noise
that droont the traffic, towards the Calton Hill.

As they rade by, it seemed the sun was shinin
brichter nor usual roun thae cantie three
that wi thon weill-kent Heid-yin had been dinin.

Nou that's the kinna thing I like to see;
tho ye and I look on and cannae jyne in,
it gies our toon some tone, ye'll all agree.

ROBERT GARIOCH

In Princes Street Gairdens

Doun by the baundstaund, by the ice-cream barrie,   *barrow*
there is a sait that says, Wilma is Fab.
Sit doun aside me here and gieze your gab,   *give me your talk*
jist you and me, a dou, and a wee cock-sparrie.   *a pigeon*

Up in the street, shop-folk sairve and harrie;   *prosperous;*
    lay slates;
weill-daean tredsmen sclate and pent and snab   *paint; cobble*
and jyne and plaister. We never let dab   *take notice*
sae lang as we can jink the strait-and-narrie.   *dodge*

A sculptured growp, classical and symbolic,
staunds by the path, maist beautiful to see:
National Savings, out for a bit frolic,

peys echt per cent til Thrift and Industry,   *to*
but dour Inflatioun, a diabolic
dou, has owrecam, and duin Thrift in the ee.

ROBERT GARIOCH

[42]

Christmas snow in Princes Street

Slush on the ground. Taxis
Go slurring by. The railing
Holds up its snowy wicks –
Beyond, the castle sails.

Pale on the dirty clouds,
High in the air, not climbing,
A second moon announces
A second sort of time.

The night shrugs distance off,
But it won't go. It whispers
Of wastes, migrations, gulfs
And swarming memories.

Here windows glow for Aladdins –
No Sesame to open
But coins that children jingle,
That taste just like the snow.

Fine to be them. But lonely
To be the tall man staring
At tinsel sprawling down
On snowfield and shambling bear

And on that globe of crimson –
Cottage where crooked women

Keep strange children for ransom;
As he in his red room

Keeps what was once his childhood.
Who will redeem it? A moment,
Only, may go by riding
And toss him his purse of gold.

What more than a moment matters –
Small wizard, whose small whisper
Lays the tall champion flat
And makes songs sing in earnest?

The high clock there, glum angel
Whose self is his own halo,
Measures off Edens; clangs
On each its sullen gate.

 – Yet still a tree of gardens
And snowy windows, rooted
Deep in a dark field,
Holds up its dangerous fruit.

And a strange will in its branches
Twinkles its scales. It hisses
Like wheels in the watery slush.
It coils in these dark minds.

And inklings grope in spaces
And breathe up from dark cellars
And lie like newspapers
Scuffed round the drinking well;

Where a drunk man, blunt lips pouting,
Sucking a thumb of water,
Is joined by a silver string
To nightblack watersheds.

NORMAN MacCAIG

Forty miles – and a whole gulf of experience – separate Edinburgh, in the east, and Glasgow, in the west. If Ruthven Todd was formed by Edinburgh, then Glasgow formed Billy Fullerton, leader of the gang known as the Brigton Billy Boys. During the 1930s, Glasgow lay in the grip of vicious criminal gangs. The Billy Boys were noisily Protestant in their allegiances, religious division being an open sore in that part of Scotland, just as it simmers below the surface today. Edwin Morgan's 'King Billy' captures the culture of the Glasgow of the time – a city that in a perverse way might revel in its violent image. The opening lines of this poem are intensely evocative – this is Glasgow, a city of greys and low skies, for all that it was the dear green place. Urban poverty, toughness, the strong loyalties, the tawdry consolation of fife bands, the sheer pointlessness of violence: these are all here in Morgan's unforgettable poem. And what an opening line: 'Grey over Riddrie the clouds piled up . . .' Morgan said that everybody seemed to remember that line; I certainly do.

Look at a picture of Billy Fullerton. Some pictures of gangsters tell us a bit more, especially if there are, as is often the case, scars to remind us of razor or knife fights. Some may be more threatening, helped by the clichés of gangster clothing. This face, though, conveys its message clearly enough: this is what is known in Glasgow as a 'hard man'. The eyes speak of his determination; the set of the mouth is one that betrays no mercy; the shaven cheeks and chin suggest a Protestant firmness. Picture the gang leader, now middle-aged, being taken to his grave in 1962. The mourners remember his glory days; as the poet says, there were some who wept.

'King Billy' is followed by 'The Starlings in George Square', another of Morgan's vivid Glasgow poems.

King Billy

Grey over Riddrie the clouds piled up,
dragged their rain through the cemetery trees.
The gates shone cold. Wind rose
flaring the hissing leaves, the branches
swung, heavy, across the lamps.
Gravestones huddled in drizzling shadow,
fickering streetlight scanned the requiescats,
a name and an urn, a date, a dove
picked out, lost, half-regained.
What is this dripping wreath, blown from its grave
red, white, blue, and gold
'To Our Leader of Thirty years Ago' –

Bareheaded, in dark suits, with flutes
and drums, they brought him here, in procession
seriously, King Billy of Brigton, dead,
from Bridgeton Cross: a memory of violence,
brooding days of empty bellies,
billiard smoke and a sour pint,
boots or fists, famous sherrickings,
the word, the scuffle, the flash, the shout,
bloody crumpling in the close,
bricks for papish windows, get
the Conks next time, the Conks ambush
the Billy Boys, the Billy Boys the Conks till
Sillitoe scuffs the razors down the stank –
No, but it isn't the violence they remember

but the legend of a violent man
born poor, gang-leader in the bad times
of idleness and boredom, lost in better days,
a bouncer in a betting club,
a quiet man at last, dying
alone in Bridgeton in a box bed.
So a thousand people stopped the traffic
for the hearse of a folk hero and the flutes
threw 'Onward Christian Soldiers' to the winds
from unironic lips, the mourners kept
in step, and there were some who wept.

Go from the grave. The shrill flutes
are silent, the march dispersed.
Deplore what is to be deplored,
and then find out the rest.

EDWIN MORGAN

The Starlings in George Square

I

Sundown on the high stonefields!
The darkening roofscape stirs
thick – alive with starlings
gathered singing in the square –
like a shower of arrows they cross
the flash of a western window,
they bead the wires with jet,
they nestle preening by the lamps
and shine, sidling by the lamps
and sing, shining, they stir
the homeward hurrying crowds.
A man looks up and points
smiling to his son beside him
wide-eyed at the clamour on those cliffs –
it sinks, shrills out in waves,
levels to a happy murmur,
scatters in swooping arcs,
a stab of confused sweetness
that pierces the boy like a story,
a story more than a song.
He will never forget that evening,
the silhouette of the roofs,
the starlings by the lamps.

II

The City Chambers are hopping mad.
Councillors with rubber plugs in their ears!
Secretaries closing windows!
Window-cleaners want protection and danger money.
The Lord Provost can't hear herself think, man.
What's that?
Lord Provost, can't hear herself think.

At the General Post Office
the clerks write Three Pounds Starling in the savings-books.
Each telephone-booth is like an aviary.
I tried to send a parcel to County Kerry but –
The cables to Cairo got fankled, sir.
What's that?
I said the cables to Cairo got fankled.

And as for the City Information Bureau –
I'm sorry I can't quite chirrup did you twit –
No I wanted to twee but perhaps you can't cheep –
Would you try once again, that's better, I – sweet –
When's the last boat to Milngavie? Tweet?
What's that?
I said when's the last boat to Milngavie?

III

There is nothing for it now but scaffolding:
clamp it together, send for the bird-men,
Scarecrow Strip for the window-ledge landings,
Cameron's Repellent on the overhead wires.
Armour our pediments against eavesdroppers.
This is a human outpost. Save our statues.
Send back the jungle. And think of the joke:
as it says in the papers, It is very comical
to watch them alight on the plastic rollers
and take a tumble. So it doesn't kill them?
All right, so who's complaining? This isn't Peking
where they shoot the sparrows for hygiene and cash.
So we're all humanitarians, locked in our cliff-dwellings
encased in our repellent, guano-free and guilt-free.
The Lord Provost sings in her marble hacienda.
The Postmaster-General licks an audible stamp.
Sir Walter is vexed that his column's deserted.
I wonder if we really deserve starlings?
There is something to be said for these joyous messengers
that we repel in our indignant orderliness.
They lift up the eyes, they lighten the heart,
and some day we'll decipher that sweet frenzied whistling
as they wheel and settle along our hard roofs
and take those grey buttresses for home.
One thing we know they say, after their fashion.
They like the warm cliffs of man.

EDWIN MORGAN

from Auld Reekie

. . . Now morn, with bonny purpie-smiles,
Kisses the air-cock o' St Giles;
Rakin their een, the servant lasses
Early begin their lies and clashes;
Ilk tells her friend o' saddest distress,
That still she brooks frae scouling mistress;
And wi her joe in turnpike stair
She'd rather snuff the stinking air,
As be subjected to her tongue,
When justly censur'd in the wrong.

    On stair wi tub, or pat in hand,
The barefoot housemaids loo to stand,
That antrin fock may ken how snell
Auld Reikie will at morning smell:
Then, with an inundation big as
The burn that 'neath the Nore Loch Brig is,
They kindly shower Edina's roses,
To quicken and regale our noses.
Now some for this, wi satire's leesh,
Hae gien auld Edinburgh a creesh:
But without souring nocht is sweet;
The morning smells that hail our street
Prepare, and gently lead the way
To simmer canty, braw and gay;
Edina's sons mair eithly share

Her spices and her dainties rare,
Than he that's never yet been call'd
Aff frae his plaidie or his fauld.

Now stairhead critics, senseless fools,
Censure their aim, and pride their rules,
In Luckenbooths, wi glowring eye,
Their neighbour's sma'est faults descry:
If ony loun should dander there,
Of aukward gate and foreign air,
They trace his steps, till they can tell
His pedigree as weel's himsel . . .

ROBERT FERGUSSON

In Honour of the City of London

London, thou art of townes *A per se*.
    Soveraign of cities, semeliest in sight,
Of high renoun, riches, and royaltie;
    Of lordis, barons, and many goodly knyght;
    Of most delectable lusty ladies bright;
Of famous prelatis in habitis clericall;
    Of merchauntis full of substaunce and myght:
London, thou art the flour of Cities all.

Gladdith anon, thou lusty Troy Novaunt,
    Citie that some tyme cleped was New Troy,
In all the erth, imperiall as thou stant,
    Pryncesse of townes, of pleasure, and of joy,
    A richer restith under no Christen roy;
For manly power, with craftis naturall,
    Fourmeth none fairer sith the flode of Noy:
London, thou art the flour of Cities all.

Gemme of all joy, jasper of jocunditie,
    Most myghty carbuncle of vertue and valour;
Strong Troy in vigour and in strenuytie;
    Of royall cities rose and geraflour;
    Empresse of townes, exalt in honour;
In beawtie beryng the crone imperiall;
    Swete paradise precelling in pleasure:
London, thow art the flour of Cities all.

Above all ryvers thy Ryver hath renowne,
    Whose beryall stremys, pleasaunt and preclare,
Under thy lusty wallys renneth down,
    Where many a swanne doth swymme with wyngis fare;
    Where many a barge doth saile, and row with are,
Where many a ship doth rest with toppe-royall.
    O! towne of townes, patrone and not-compare:
London, thou art the flour of Cities all.

Upon thy lusty Brigge of pylers white
    Been merchauntis full royall to behold;
Upon thy stretis goth many a semely knyght
    In velvet gownes and cheynes of fyne gold.
    By Julyus Cesar thy Tour founded of old
May be the hous of Mars victoryall,
    Whose artillary with tonge may not be told:
London, thou art the flour of Cities all.

Strong be thy wallis that about the standis;
    Wise be the people that within the dwellis;
Fresh is thy ryver with his lusty strandis;
    Blith be thy chirches, wele sownyng be thy bellis;
    Riche be thy merchauntis in substaunce that excellis;
Fair be thy wives, right lovesom, white and small;
    Clere be thy virgyns, lusty under kellis:
London, thow art the flour of Cities all.

Thy famous Maire, by pryncely governaunce,
    With swerd of justice the rulith prudently.

No Lord of Parys, Venyce, or Floraunce
    In dignytie or honoure goeth to hym nye.
    He is exampler, loode-ster, and guye;
Principall patrone and roose orygynalle,
    Above all Maires as maister moost worthy:
London, thou art the flour of Cities all.

WILLIAM DUNBAR

The Night City

Unmet at Euston in a dream
Of London under Turner's steam
Misting the iron gantries, I
Found myself running away
From Scotland into the golden city.

I ran down Gray's Inn Road and ran
Till I was under a black bridge.
This was me at nineteen
Late at night arriving between
The buildings of the City of London.

And then I (O I have fallen down)
Fell in my dream beside the Bank
Of England's wall to bed, me
With my money belt of Northern ice.
I found Eliot and he said yes

And sprang into a Holmes cab.
Boswell passed me in the fog
Going to visit Whistler who
Was with John Donne who had just seen
Paul Potts shouting on Soho Green.

Midnight. I hear the moon
Light chiming on St Paul's.

The City is empty. Night
Watchmen are drinking their tea.

The Fire had burnt out.
The Plague's pits had closed
And gone into literature.

Between the big buildings
I sat like a flea crouched
In the stopped works of a watch.

W.S. GRAHAM

Freedom Come-All-Ye

Roch the wind in the clear day's dawin
    Blaws the cloods heelster-gowdie ow'r the bay,
But there's mair nor a roch wind blawin
    Through the great glen o' the warld the day.
It's a thocht that will gar oor rottans
    – A' they rogues that gang gallus, fresh and gay –
Tak the road, and seek ither loanins
    For their ill ploys, tae sport and play

Nae mair will the bonnie callants
    Mairch tae war when oor braggarts crousely craw,
Nor wee weans frae pit-heid and clachan
    Mourn the ships sailin' doon the Broomielaw.
Broken faimlies in lands we've herriet,
    Will curse Scotland the Brave nae mair, nae mair;
Black and white, ane til ither mairriet,
    Mak the vile barracks o' their maisters bare.

So come all ye at hame wi' Freedom,
    Never heed whit the hoodies croak for doom.
In your hoose a' the bairns o' Adam
    Can find breid, barley-bree and painted room.
When MacLean meets wi's freens in Springburn
    A' the roses and geans will turn tae bloom,
And a black boy frae yont Nyanga
    Dings the fell gallows o' the burghers doon.

HAMISH HENDERSON

Islands

Hugh MacDiarmid observed in his book *The Islands of Scotland* that an island is 'an almost startlingly entire thing, in these days of the subdivision, the atomisation of life'. An island is indeed a microcosm of the larger world, complete unto itself. Islands are places to which the outsider must travel; islands have their way of doing things; they have their perspective. They are often beautiful; they are often peaceful in a way in which the mainland is not. In Scotland, islands are places of beauty and of poetry, of memories and of dreams. Not surprisingly, there are numerous island poems, and one of the most famous of these is Hugh MacDiarmid's poignant 'Island Funeral', the measured beat of which is grave and beautiful.

Island Funeral

The procession winds like a little snake
Between the walls of irregular grey stones
Piled carelessly on one another.
Sometimes, on this winding track,
The leaders are doubled back
Quite near us.

It is a grey world, sea and sky
Are colourless as the grey stones,
And the small fields are hidden by the walls
That fence them on every side.

See in perspective, the walls
Overlap each other

As far as the skyline on the hill,
Hiding every blade of grass between them,
So that all the island appears
One jumble of grey boulders.
The last grey wall outlined on the sky
Has the traceried effect
Of a hedge of thorn in winter.

The men in the stiff materials
Of their homespun clothes
Look like figures cut from cardboard,
But shod in their rawhide rivelins
They walk with the springing step of mountaineers.
The women wear black shawls
And black crimson skirts.

A line of tawny seaweed fringes the bay
Between high-water mark and low.

It is luminous between the grey of rocky shore
And the grey of sullen water.

HUGH MacDIARMID

George Mackay Brown wrote about Orkney, and that, of course, is very different from the world of Scotland's western islands. Orkney is a place of cultivation as much as it is of fishing. Its history is different. Hebridean islands were in the orbit of Ireland; Orkney still feels Norse.

'Beachcomber' refers to a day when the harvest of the sea was exciting and exotic. Today it is plastic. And that chimes with two lines in the second of these poems, 'Hamnavoe'. The poet writes: 'And because, under equality's sun, / All things wear now to a common soiling . . .' These lines might refer to the flattening effect of modern culture, where difference and colour, as well as character, are eroded by the bland and the international.

Beachcomber

Monday I found a boot –
Rust and salt leather.
I gave it back to the sea, to dance in.

Tuesday a spar of timber worth thirty bob.
Next winter
It will be a chair, a coffin, a bed.

Wednesday a half can of Swedish spirits.
I tilted my head.
The shore was cold with mermaids and angels.

Thursday I got nothing, seaweed,
A whale bone,
Wet feet and a loud cough.

Friday I held a seaman's skull,
Sand spilling from it
The way time is told on kirkyard stones.

Saturday a barrel of sodden oranges.
A Spanish ship
Was wrecked last month at The Kame.

Sunday, for fear of the elders,
I sit on my bum.
What's heaven? A sea chest with a thousand gold coins.

GEORGE MACKAY BROWN

Hamnavoe

My father passed with his penny letters
Through closes opening and shutting like legends
    When barbarous with gulls
    Hamnavoe's morning broke

On the salt and tar steps. Herring boats,
Puffing red sails, the tillers
    Of cold horizons, leaned
    Down the gull-gaunt tide

And threw dark nets on sudden silver harvests.
A stallion at the sweet fountain
    Dredged water, and touched
    Fire from steel-kissed cobbles.

Hard on noon four bearded merchants
Past the pipe-spitting pier-head strolled,
    Holy with greed, chanting
    Their slow grave jargon.

A tinker keened like a tartan gull
At cuithe-hung doors. A crofter lass
    Trudged through the lavish dung
    In a dream of cornstalks and milk.

Blessings and soup plates circled. Euclidian light
Ruled the town in segments blue and gray.
    The school bell yawned and lisped
    Down ignorant closes.

In 'The Arctic Whaler' three blue elbows fell,
Regular as waves, from beards spumy with porter,
    Till the amber day ebbed out
    To its black dregs.

The boats drove furrows homeward, like ploughmen
In blizzards of gulls. Gaelic fisher girls
    Flashed knife and dirge
    Over drifts of herring,

And boys with penny wands lured gleams
From the tangled veins of the flood. Houses went blind
    Up one steep close, for a
    Grief by the shrouded nets.

The kirk, in a gale of psalms, went heaving through
A tumult of roofs, freighted for heaven. And lovers
    Unblessed by steeples, lay under
    The buttered bannock of the moon.

He quenched his lantern, leaving the last door.
Because of his gay poverty that kept
    My seapink innocence
    From the worm and black wind;

And because, under equality's sun,
All things wear now to a common soiling,
  In the fire of images
  Gladly I put my hand
  To save that day for him.

GEORGE MACKAY BROWN

When I was nineteen, or thereabouts, I went to the Outer Isles one summer. It was June, and there was virtually no darkness at night. There was the machair and the green sea beyond. The air was filled with that indescribable smell of that edge of Scotland – a smell of water and seaweed and peat and the wind from the sea. Tessa Ransford describes that all so well in 'Nocturne Lewis'. You can't close your eyes while reading a poem, but close them after reading this and you will see the island.

Nocturne Lewis

It is raining on Lewis in the night;
darkness has brimmed over the hills
spilling upon the moor
and dropping into circles of inland sea.

Last night the moon was wildly shed
by mountain and cloud to reveal a sheer
countenance at the window
and blending with the water in bright festoons

but tonight the dark is raining on Lewis
on the black-house with its hunched thatch
on battered abandoned buses
derelict cars and stacks of murky peat.

Boats are plying under the rain
and enormous eels under the boats
and fishing nets are lifted
up and under the tide like diving birds.

For thousands of years of nights the stones
have loomed in lonely communion
beneath the moon, the rain,
ritually aloof, cleansed and illumined

and the white schist of my lasting self
safe and awake yet exposed to love –
its darkness and shafts of light –
takes up position in line with primeval wisdom.

TESSA RANSFORD

Here are two poems by Sorley MacLean, the greatest Gaelic poet of our times. 'The Choice' is about commitment and immersion in the cause that is life. 'Hallaig' is about the disappearance of a culture and the people who sustained it. The scars of the Highland Clearances, that great act of brutality perpetrated on the Highlands of Scotland, have never fully healed – the effect of that dreadful chapter in Scottish history is still evident, not only in deserted townships, but also in the current difficulties that people in those depopulated areas have in keeping communities alive. 'The dead have been seen alive' is a particularly powerful line.

An Roghainn

Choisich mi cuide ri mo thuigse
a-muigh ri taobh a' chuain;
bha sinn còmhla ach bha ise
a' fuireach tiotan bhuam.

An sin thionndaidh i ag ràdha:
a bheil e fìor gun cual
thu gu bheil do ghaol geal àlainn
a' pòsadh tràth Di-luain?

Bhac mi 'n cridhe bha 'g éirigh
'nam bhroilleach reubte luath
is thubhairt mi: tha mi cinnteach;
carson bu bhriag e bhuam?

Ciamar a smaoinichinn gun glacainn
an rionnag leugach òir,
gum beirinn oirre 's gun cuirinn i
gu ciallach 'na mo phòc?

Cha d' ghabh mise bàs croinn-ceusaidh
an éiginn chruaidh na Spàinn
is ciamar sin bhiodh dùil agam
ri aon duais ùir an dàin?

Cha do lean mi ach an t-slighe chrìon
bheag ìosal thioram thlàth,
is ciamar sin a choinnichinn
ri beithir-theine ghràidh?

The Choice

I walked with my reason
out beside the sea.
We were together but it was
keeping a little distance from me.

Then it turned saying:
is it true you heard
that your beautiful white love
is getting married early on Monday?

I checked the heart that was rising
in my torn swift breast
and I said: most likely;
why should I lie about it?

How should I think that I would grab
the radiant golden star,
that I would catch it and put it
prudently in my pocket?

I did not take a cross's death
in the hard extremity of Spain
and how then should I expect
the one new prize of fate?

I followed only a way
that was small, mean, low, dry, lukewarm,
and how then should I meet
the thunderbolt of love?

Ach nan robh 'n roghainn rithist dhomh
's mi 'm sheasamh air an àird,
leumainn à nèamh no iutharna
le spiorad 's cridhe slàn.

SOMHAIRLE MacGILL-EAIN

But if I had the choice again
and stood on that headland,
I would leap from heaven or hell
with a whole spirit and heart.

SORLEY MacLEAN

Hallaig

'Tha tìm, am fiadh, an coille Hallaig'

Tha bùird is tàirnean air an uinneig
troimh 'm faca mi an Aird an Iar
's tha mo ghaol aig Allt Hallaig
'na craoibh beithe, 's bha i riamh

eadar an t-Inbhir 's Poll a' Bhainne,
thall 's a bhos mu Bhaile-Chùirn:
tha i 'na beithe, 'na calltuinn,
'na caorunn dhìreach sheang ùir.

Ann an Screapadal mo chinnidh,
far robh Tarmad 's Eachann Mòr,
tha 'n nigheanan 's am mic 'nan coille
a' gabhail suas ri taobh an lòin.

Uaibhreach a nochd na coilich ghiuthais
a' gairm air mullach Cnoc an Rà,
dìreach an druim ris a' ghealaich –
chan iadsan coille mo ghràidh.

Fuirichidh mi ris a' bheithe
gus an tig i mach an Càrn,
gus am bi am bearradh uile
o Bheinn na Lice f' a sgàil.

Hallaig

'Time, the deer, is in the wood of Hallaig'

The window is nailed and boarded
through which I saw the West
and my love is at the Burn of Hallaig,
a birch tree, and she has always been

between Inver and Milk Hollow,
here and there about Baile-chuirn:
she is a birch, a hazel,
a straight, slender young rowan.

In Screapadal of my people,
where Norman and Big Hector were,
their daughters and their sons are a wood
going up beside the stream.

Proud tonight the pine cocks
crowing on the top of Cnoc an Ra,
straight their backs in the moonlight –
they are not the wood I love.

I will wait for the birch wood
until it comes up by the cairn,
until the whole ridge from Beinn na Lice
will be under its shade.

Mura tig 's ann theàrnas mi a Hallaig,
a dh'ionnsaigh sàbaid nam marbh,
far a bheil an sluagh a' tathaich,
gach aon ghinealach a dh'fhalbh.

Tha iad fhathast ann a Hallaig,
Clann Ghill-Eain 's Clann MhicLeòid,
na bh' ann ri linn Mhic Ghille Chaluim:
chunnacas na mairbh beò.

Na fir 'nan laighe air an lèanaig
aig ceann gach taighe a bh' ann,
na h-igheanan 'nan coille bheithe,
dìreach an druim, crom an ceann.

Eadar an Leac is na Feàrnaibh
tha 'n rathad mòr fo chòinnich chiùin,
's na h-igheanan 'nam badan sàmhach
a' dol a Chlachan mar o thùs.

Agus a' tilleadh às a' Chlachan,
à Suidhisnis 's à tìr nam beò;
a chuile tè òg uallach,
gun bhristeadh cridhe an sgeòil.

O Allt na Feàrnaibh gus an fhaoilinn
tha soilleir an dìomhaireachd nam beann
chan eil ach coimhthional nan nighean
a' cumail na coiseachd gun cheann.

If it does not, I will go down to Hallaig,
to the Sabbath of the dead,
where the people are frequenting,
every single generation gone.

They are still in Hallaig,
MacLeans and MacLeods,
all who were there in the time of Mac Gille Chaluim:
the dead have been seen alive.

The men lying on the green
at the end of every house that was,
the girls a wood of birches,
straight their backs, bent their heads.

Between the Leac and Fearns
the road is under mild moss
and the girls in silent bands
go to Clachan as in the beginning,

and return from Clachan,
from Suisnish and the land of the living;
each one young and light-stepping,
without the heartbreak of the tale.

From the Burn of Fearns to the raised beach
that is clear in the mystery of the hills,
there is only the congregation of the girls
keeping up the endless walk,

A' tilleadh a Hallaig anns an fheasgar,
anns a' chamhanaich bhalbh bheò,
a' lìonadh nan leathadan casa,
an gàireachdaich 'nam chluais 'na ceò,

's am bòidhche 'na sgleò air mo chridhe
mun tig an ciaradh air na caoil,
's nuair theàrnas grian air cùl Dhùn Cana
thig peileir dian à gunna Ghaoil;

's buailear am fiadh a tha 'na thuaineal
a' snòtach nan làraichean feòir;
thig reothadh air a shùil sa choille:
chan fhaighear lorg air fhuil ri in' bheò.

SOMHAIRLE MacGILL-EAIN

coming back to Hallaig in the evening,
in the dumb living twilight,
filling the steep slopes,
their laughter a mist in my ears,

and their beauty a film on my heart
before the dimness comes on the kyles,
and when the sun goes down behind Dun Cana
a vehement bullet will come from the gun of Love;

and will strike the deer that goes dizzily,
sniffing at the grass-grown ruined homes;
his eye will freeze in the wood,
his blood will not be traced while I live.

SORLEY MacLEAN

George Bruce was born and brought up in the North East of Scotland. The sea and its shore play a major role in his poetry. He often talks about that memory, common to us all, of walking in the sand, feeling the sea at our feet. These three poems resonate with me for different reasons. 'Shetland and Ponies' does so because in my student days in Edinburgh I used to spend university breaks with an aunt on the island of Unst. Ponies were everywhere. The land was marked by peat cuttings – and I learned how to stack peat. The only way of getting there was by steamer from Aberdeen to Lerwick, and then by much smaller steamer, from Lerwick to Uyeasound, the last part of the journey being by a tiny boat with an outboard engine. My aunt collected me from the pier in her ancient Lea-Francis motor car. Everybody knew who you were and why you were there. At New Year, the school bus was lost for some time because the driver had enjoyed himself too much and had forgotten where he had left it. It was a different world.

Shetland and Ponies

Light – when you come to this place –
light is falling from the sky
and the water is returning it;
the land, wrinkled and dark, a dead skin
that might crack open with no sound
and the bright water drain into that breathless dark,
lost like a single life in emptiness,
and not a tree to bless with its gentle growth,
but the bone of the world pressing through,

the stone face to which the human face returns.
Inhospitable but splendid – this North land
that tells the cosmic tale
of earth and sky and water.

Water – in the beginning a drop of water
and the light was in the water and there
each stone was shaped to be itself and none other,
each shell to be itself and none other,
each creature to be itself and none other,
peerie fish and crab and whale
seen and known and named,
yet unknown as the round of the sea.

I look in the glass that is water
And know I am a stranger to this place
I look into light upon light
And know it is not of me.
I look on to the waste of land.
I do not belong, but these

fourlegs make the spaces their own,
a backyard for their games,
a stamping ground for their romp
a prancing place for their pride.
They populate it with their warmth,
make jokes about the mountains –
this universe is their home.

GEORGE BRUCE

Voyage We to Islands

Here is no continuing city
Voyage we then to islands in this
Flux of time and tide
And listen hoping for news beyond
Tide and time, and taste,
Anticipating the luscious long asked for
Fruit never withdrawn nor rotting.
A sun shines – but where?

From prints upon the brain,
Effluent into light, the tender past –
That seen by my childhood's eyes,
That which has long since withdrawn
On an ebb – flows now.
The rocking horse with glazed eye stares,
The cuckoo clock calls,
Its door shuts – these, part of a
Once for ever world, now once
Upon a time – gone with
The silver gong's stroke, fallen
From permanence.

Voyage we for islands securely pebbled,
Holding the boat's jar, time resistant,
With water diamonded under a white sun.
But where?

GEORGE BRUCE

An Island and Seals

Old grey heads, curious and stupid like the old
They came about our anchored boat
Wondering at us visitors to their ancient world
Of tides and beaches peopled with fish and birds.
On the white sands the spindly oyster catchers,
In the shallows the frantic terns,
Above the mast the heavy black-backed gulls –
All considered us, took our measure.

Every would-be traveller – and who is not?
Must at the first dawn-streaked sky
Step with hope – or heartless – East, West, South or North.
Seas are between, land or doubtful sky
And painful traverse sets in motion
Heart beats to an ancient tune. Time
For a departure. O Time! One it is alleged
Once sought successfully but with too much pain.

There was a pause, a cessation of motion,
A pause in the bobbing grey heads, a pause
In the motion of water. Light fixed
The red-legged oyster catchers, caught
Black-capped tern and lumbering gull
In an equipoise. We looked beyond
To island upon island linked in the long
Glittering of waters – wondering where?

Now in the years between I doubt
If all was well on that bright day.

Had we but kept the bounded measure,
Ceased from willing, observation, conversation
With the self and with another,
Had we but simply been at leisure
In that suspense of fish and bird and sea
And with the old grey-headed seals – what then?

GEORGE BRUCE

Before we leave islands, there is one island poem that is utterly irreverent, but extremely funny. Some people may find it too dyspeptic, but I think its dyspepsia is gorgeous, and puts it in the front rank of dyspeptic poems. Hamish Blair, the reputed author of this poem, was a naval officer stationed at Scapa Flow during the Second World War. He did not appear to have enjoyed the experience.

Bloody Orkney

This bloody town's a bloody cuss,
No bloody trains, no bloody bus,
And no one cares for bloody us
In bloody Orkney.

The bloody roads are bloody bad,
The bloody folks are bloody mad,
They'd make the brightest bloody sad,
In bloody Orkney.

All bloody clouds, and bloody rains,
No bloody kerbs, no bloody drains,
The Council's got no bloody brains,
In bloody Orkney.

Everything's so bloody dear,
A bloody bob, for bloody beer,
And is it good? – no bloody fear,
In bloody Orkney.

The bloody 'flicks' are bloody old,
The bloody seats are bloody cold,
You can't get in for bloody gold
In bloody Orkney.

The bloody dances make you smile,
The bloody band is bloody vile,
It only cramps your bloody style,
In bloody Orkney.

No bloody sport, no bloody games,
No bloody fun, the bloody dames
Won't even give their bloody names
In bloody Orkney.

Best bloody place is bloody bed,
With bloody ice on bloody head,
You might as well be bloody dead,
In bloody Orkney.

There's nothing greets your bloody eye
But bloody sea and bloody sky,
'Roll on demob!' we bloody cry
In bloody Orkney.

HAMISH BLAIR

Anybody who has visited Orkney will know that this poem is a travesty of the truth. Orkney is a beguiling place and does not deserve this nonsense. Fortunately, the Orcadians had the last laugh, as one of their number is said to have composed this robust response:

> Captain Hamish Bloody Blair,
> Isna posted here nae mare,
> But no one seems to bloody care
> In bloody Orkney.

Childhood

Robert Louis Stevenson is perhaps the most continuously popular Scottish writer of the nineteenth century. The author of *Kidnapped* and *Treasure Island*, Stevenson was at heart an adventurer. He had a particular sympathy for and understanding of childhood. His collection of poems, *A Child's Garden of Verses*, continues to be in print and is still much loved by many readers. Poetry about childhood can easily become sentimental, but Stevenson avoids this, managing to convey with effortless delicacy, the sense of wonder that we all recall from childhood. One wonders whether the highly sophisticated, media-savvy children of current times – children brought up attached to their electronic devices – feel that awe in the face of what the world has to offer. Possibly not. They may well have seen it all by the time they are six.

Here is Stevenson showing an understanding of infantile psychology. Very young children do not share their toys; older ones, and adults, are often the same.

Looking Forward

When I am grown to man's estate
I shall be very proud and great,
And tell the other girls and boys
Not to meddle with my toys.

ROBERT LOUIS STEVENSON

Ideas of how children should behave have changed radically. Stevenson has his tongue in cheek here, but what modern parent, exhausted at the end of a day of child care, may not get pleasure from these lines, and sigh.

The Whole Duty of Children

A child should always say what's true
And speak when he is spoken to,
And behave mannerly at table;
At least as far as he is able.

ROBERT LOUIS STEVENSON

Stevenson was a sickly child who spent a great deal of time confined to the sickroom. From his room he saw the lamplighter, Leerie as he was known, going about his business. You can still see the lamp outside Stevenson's house in Edinburgh's Heriot Row to this day.

The Lamplighter

My tea is nearly ready and the sun has left the sky;
It's time to take the window to see Leerie going by;
For every night at teatime and before you take your seat,
With lantern and with ladder he comes posting up the
    street.

Now Tom would be a driver and Maria go to sea,
And my papa's a banker and as rich as he can be;
But I, when I am stronger and can choose what I'm to do,
Oh Leerie, I'll go round at night and light the lamps with
    you!

For we are very lucky, with a lamp before the door,
And Leerie stops to light it as he lights so many more;
And O! before you hurry by with ladder and with light,
O Leerie, see a little child and nod to him tonight!

ROBERT LOUIS STEVENSON

Like Stevenson, William Soutar struggled with illness. He was born in Perth in 1898, and was old enough to go into the navy during the last two years of the First World War. He studied briefly at Edinburgh University but was dogged by a serious arthritic illness and became bed-ridden at the age of thirty. He died of tuberculosis in 1943. He had a difficult life, but it did not prevent him from writing a considerable body of poetry, including numerous five-line poems, cinquains, that he called epigrams. The poem below, 'Winter's Awa', is an octave and is typical of the brief, highly descriptive poems that Soutar liked to compose for children.

Winter's Awa

Noo the snaw creeps fae the braes
And is gaen:
Noo the trees clap on their claes
Ane be ane:
Yonder owre the windy muir
Flees the craw;
And cries into the caller air,
Winter's awa!

WILLIAM SOUTAR

Memories of childhood in a country like Scotland are not surprisingly mixed up with recollections of beaches and the sea. Edwin Muir and George Bruce, poets associated with Orkney and the North East respectively, employ such images in their invocation of childhood as a time of discovery and intense feeling.

Childhood

Long time he lay upon the sunny hill,
   To his father's house below securely bound.
Far off the silent, changing sound was still,
  With the black islands lying thick around.

He saw each separate height, each vaguer hue,
   Where the massed islands rolled in mist away,
And though all ran together in his view
   He knew that unseen straits between them lay.

Often he wondered what new shores were there.
   In thought he saw the still light on the sand,
The shallow water clear in tranquil air,
  And walked through it in joy from strand to strand.

Over the sound a ship so slow would pass
   That in the black hill's gloom it seemed to lie.

The evening sound was smooth like sunken glass,
    And time seemed finished ere the ship passed by.

Grey tiny rocks slept round him where he lay,
    Moveless as they, more still as evening came,
The grasses threw straight shadows far away,
    And from the house his mother called his name.

EDWIN MUIR

Child on the Beach

On the shore a child picked up
The bleached skull of a rabbit,
Noted the empty eye socket,
Then ran with his joy
Till this dead shell halted
His step to hear at his ear
Miracles shout from cavities
That contained seas at work.

But age picked on me that day.
The ear was blank at that hole.
The dance of all the fishes stopped,
The tern dived oh not for fun,
The sea shrunk grey and unimportant.
Listen, be attentive to the years.
Note the thin bone structure,
Salt entered the eyeholes
To make this new thing.

GEORGE BRUCE

The Child and the Sea

I. THE BETRAYAL

But the firm sand betrayed her
And the ball spinning was caught
By the shivering sea.
Treacherous it danced her heart
Took it to its perplexity in an endless
Time streaming horizonwards.

Nor would again the flaunting sun
Tell truths of happiness to be,
Nor would those disturbed waters
Entrusted with a hundred confidences
Receive her benediction; kindnesses
Would not grow from her lips again.

The dream was taken from her.
She was no more herself. Once
The blue pebbles at the edge
Of the lemonade sea were sweets.
How many years had it held
In hiding this unsupportable moment.

2. SHE REBUKES THE SEA

O my love, once you were tremendous
With a billion wonders to tell,
Tell me of tales of thin finned
Angels that went about my
Pearly feet in the sand
That snuggled the brazen
Faced crabs with pop-eyes.
Once, my love, you sent
The bubbles gold-eyed to the top.
Salt you were, you, more blissful
Than candies with your sharp
Tongue. But you
Were with the unkind Time
That took the world
To the grudging night.

GEORGE BRUCE

Boys Among Rock Pools

Boys on knees, or prostrate, and scrambling
About rocks, by rock pools and inlets,
Noting with accurate eye the wash of water.
They hunt (O primitives!) for small fish,
Inches long only, and quicksilver,
But pink beneath the dorsal fin
Moving with superb locomotion.
Bodies bent, eyes all upon the prey –
Boys in shallow water with sun-warmed feet.

GEORGE BRUCE

Countryside & Animals

There is a view, explored by the critic Stuart Kelly, that Sir Walter Scott invented Scotland. There is much to be said for this: Scott was certainly the creator of a whole genre of historical fiction, and the romantic idea of Scotland, so powerful in the European imagination of the nineteenth century, owed a great deal to his vision. This was expressed in both his voluminous novels and in his similarly voluminous poetry. Here is a brief example of Scott's romanticism:

Proud Maisie

Proud Maisie is in the wood,
    Walking so early;
Sweet Robin sits on the bush,
    Singing so rarely.

'Tell me, thou bonny bird,
    When shall I marry me?' –
'When six braw gentlemen
Kirkward shall carry ye.'

'Who makes the bridal bed,
    Birdie, say truly?' –
'The grey-headed sexton
    That delves the grave duly.

'The glowworm o'er grave and stone
    Shall light thee steady;
The owl from the steeple sing,
    "Welcome, proud lady." '

SIR WALTER SCOTT

Robert Burns was the author of a famous poem about dogs: 'The Twa Dogs'. That was anthropomorphic, of course, as it consisted in a dialogue between two tykes, Caesar and Luath. There is no such anthropomorphism in Burns' famous mouse poem, one of the most moving and lyrical of his works. This poem is usually referred to as 'To a Mouse', although the full title appends to that – 'On Turning Her Up in Her Nest with the Plough, November 1785'. This poem has the distinction of containing two lines that have passed into popular aphorism, often quoted when things go wrong. These words say everything that needs to be said about human failure and its inevitability: 'The best laid schemes of *Mice* an' *Men*, / Gang aft agley'. These lines are to hand whenever we contemplate the frustration of our carefully planned projects, ranging from the major – the explosion of an expensive rocket on the launch pad – to the minor – the collapse of a soufflé in the kitchen. They have a calming, almost fatalistic effect. Do not fret, for these things happen. I told you so. Do not be too confident that things will work out as you want them to work out. Do not get above yourself. And perhaps most importantly, do not be too quick to blame others when things go wrong.

But there is so much more to the poem. There is the pitiful image of the tiny mouse disturbed by the terrifying plough. Who amongst us has not seen a mouse scurrying away, cowered, when we surprise it in the pantry or the kitchen? How large we are; how small it is. How neat and perfect its form against the threatening human giant. And if we sense this and feel sorry that we and the mouse are on different sides of a battle, then there may come to mind perhaps the most arresting lines in the entire poem: 'I'm truly sorry Man's Dominion/ Has broken Nature's social union'. These lines sometimes occur to me when I inadvertently step on a small scurrying insect, and even when that sort of thing happens deliberately: we are quite large creatures, and inevitably we crush smaller beings living their lives at ground level. Recently, camping in the Snowy Mountains of Australia, I had to visit, as all must do, the outside privy in a remote campsite. In Australia such outbuildings are called the 'dunny', and there are all sorts of stories about the wildlife that may be encountered in a rural dunny. They are the haunt of brown snakes and redback spiders, both of which can do a great deal of damage to any human they encounter. Dunny stories are calculated to put you off paying a necessary visit, and yet eventually courage must be built up for the test. In my case, I discovered the dunny populated by fairly large biting ants – if not a small army of them, then at least a platoon. As I brushed them off the seat, sending them into some frightful deep hole beneath, those lines of Burns occurred to me; indeed we can be sorry for the things we have to do as much as for the things we do by mistake.

At the end of this poem, of course, Burns makes an observation about the cost of awareness. As humans we can reflect on our past and imagine our future – both of which activities may involve discomfort, even dread. A mouse cannot do that and is, perhaps, more blessed than we are for that very reason.

To a Mouse, On Turning Her Up in Her Nest with the Plough, November 1785

Wee, sleekit, cowran, tim'rous beastie,   *furtive; cowering*
O, what a panic's in thy breastie!
Thou need na start awa sae hasty,
       Wi' bickering brattle!   *noisy rushing*
I wad be laith to rin an' chase thee,
       Wi' murd'ring *pattle*!   *plough-cleaning spade*

I'm truly sorry Man's dominion
Has broken Nature's social union,
An' justifies that ill opinion,
       Which makes thee startle,
At me, thy poor, earth-born companion,
       An' *fellow-mortal*!

I doubt na, whyles, but thou may thieve;   *sometimes*
What then? poor beastie, thou maun live!   *must*
A *daimen-icker* in a *thrave*   *ear of corn; stack of grain*
       'S a sma' request:
I'll get a blessin wi' the lave,   *rest*
       An' never miss't!

Thy wee-bit *housie*, too, in ruin!
It's silly wa's the win's are strewin!   *walls*
An' naething, now, to big a new ane,   *build*
       O' foggage green!   *rank grass*
An' bleak December's winds ensuin,
       Baith snell an' keen!   *sharp*

Thou saw the fields laid bare an' wast,
An' weary Winter comin fast,
An' cozie here, beneath the blast,
      Thou thought to dwell,
Till crash! the cruel *coulter* past   *ploughshare*
      Out thro' thy cell.

That wee-bit heap o' leaves an' stibble,
Has cost thee monie a weary nibble!
Now thou's turn'd out, for a' thy trouble,
      But house or hald,   *without*
To thole the Winter's sleety dribble,   *endure*
      An' *cranreuch* cauld!   *hoar-frost*

But Mousie, thou are no thy lane,
In proving *foresight* may be vain:
The best-laid schemes o' *Mice* an' *Men*
      Gang aft agley,   *awry*
An' lea'e us nought but grief an' pain,
  For promis'd joy!

Still, thou art blest, compared wi' *me*!
The present only toucheth thee:
But Och! I *backward* cast my e'e,
      On prospects drear!
An' *forward*, tho' I canna *see*,
  – I guess an' *fear*!

ROBERT BURNS

The original Scots Makars were poets of the fifteenth and sixteenth centuries, including Robert Henryson. Henryson is best known for three long poems that he wrote, one of which is an adaptation of Aesop's Fables. It is in this poem that we find his charming 'The Taill of the Uponlandis Mous and the Burges Mous'. This is the story of the town mouse and the country mouse – a universal theme. It is the story of the innocent in the big city, the underlying plot of so many novels, plays, and poems in just about every culture. It is very familiar.

There is a very firm moral in this poem: the grass is not always greener; stick to what you know; be content with what you have. What a seditious message that is in a consumer society where we are encouraged to do exactly the opposite. We are told to buy new things that we do not need. We are encouraged to follow fashion. We are made to think the less of ourselves if we fail to join in the spending frenzy. This poem is a hymn to the virtues of the simple life and of staying in touch with the source of that which we use to clothe and feed ourselves. It could also be a parable on place: our sense of place has been grossly disrupted by the restlessness of the modern world, by the easy movement of peoples, by the destruction of local culture. We feel the consequences of that disruption, that fracturing, in heightened unhappiness.

The country mouse in Henryson's poem has a diet that would meet with approval of a real food enthusiast today: it includes (in the original Scots spellings) *corne, ry, nuttis, peis* and *beinis.* By contrast, her sophisticated urban counterpart is heading for coronary artery disease by choosing *cheis, butter, mutoun* and *beif.*

The Two Mice

Esope, myne authour, makis mentioun   *Aesop*
Of twa myis, and thay wer sisteris deir,
Of quham the eldest duelt in ane borous toun;   *whom; burgh*
The uther wynnit uponland weill neir,   *dwelt in the country*
Richt soliter, quhyle under busk and breir,   *alone; sometimes; bush; briar*
Quhilis in the corne, in uther mennis skaith,   *men's harm*
As owtlawis dois and levis on thair waith.   *lived; plunder*

This rurall mous in to the wynter tyde   *time*
Had hunger, cauld, and tholit grit distres;   *endured*
The uther mous, that in the burgh can byde,   *lived*
Was gild brother and made ane fre burges,   *guild; citizen of the burgh*
Toll-fre als, but custum mair or les,   *tax-free*
And fredome had to ga quhair ever scho list   *she*
Amang the cheis and meill, in ark and kist.   *cheese; meal; container; chest*

Ane tyme quhein scho wes full and unfute-sair,   *not footsore*
Scho tuke in mynd hir sister upon land,
And langit for to heir of hir weilfair,
To se quhat lyfe scho led under the wand.   *branch*
Bairfute allone, with pykestaf in hir hand,
As pure pylgryme, scho passit owt off town
To seik hir sister, baith ovre daill and down.

Throw mony wilsum wayis can scho walk,
Throw mosse and mure, throw bankis, busk, and breir,   *bog; moor*
Fra fur to fur, cryand fra balk to balk,   *furrow; ridge*
'Cum furth to me, my awin sister deir!

Cry peip anis!' With that the mous culd heir   *once*
And knew hir voce, as kinnisman will do   *kinsfolk*
Be verray kynd, and furth scho come hir to.   *naturally*

The hartlie cheir, Lord God! geve ye had sene   *heartfelt; if*
Beis kith quhen that thir sisteris met,   *is shown*
And grit kyndnes wes schawin thame betuene,   *showing*
For quhylis thay leuch, and quhylis for joy thay gret,   *laughed; wept*
Quhyle kissit sweit, quhylis in armis plet,   *embraced*
And thus thay fure quhill soberit wes their mude;   *behaved; until; sobered*
Syne fute for fute unto the chalmer yude.   *then; chamber; went*

As I hard say, it was ane semple wane,   *heard; humble; dwelling*
Off fog and farne full misterlyk wes maid,   *moss and fern; poverty*
Ane sillie scheill under ane erdfast stane,   *simple hovel*
Off quhilk the entres wes not hie nor braid;   *which; entrance*
And in the samin thay went, but mair abaid,   *without further delay*
Withoutin fyre or candill birnand bricht,   *burning brightly*
For comonly sic pykeris luffis not lycht.   *thieves do not love light*

Quhen thay wer lugit thus, thir sely myse,   *lodged; simple*
The youngest sister into hir butterie hyid,   *larder; hastened*
And brocht furth nuttis and peis, in steid off spyce;   *brought out; peas*
Giff this wes gude fair, I do it on thame besyde.   *good fare*
This burges mous prunyit forth in pryde,   *town mouse; burst out*
And said, 'Sister, is this your dayly fude?'   *food*
'Quhy not,' quod scho, 'is not this meit rycht gude?'   *why; said; food*

'Na, be my saull, I think it bot ane scorne.'   *soul; insult*
'Madame,' quod scho, 'ye be the mair to blame.

My mother sayd, efter that we wer borne,
That I and ye lay baith within ane wame;   *one womb*
I keip the ryte and custome off my dame,   *standard; mother*
And off my syre, levand in povertie,   *father; living*
For landis have we nane in propertie.'   *possession*

'My fair sister,' quod scho, 'have me excusit;
This rude dyat and I can not accord.   *rough diet*
To tender meit my stomok is ay usit,   *delicate food; accustomed*
For quhy I fair als weill as ony lord.   *because; fare*
Thir wydderit peis and nuttis, or thay be bord,   *withered; before; pierced*
Wil brek my teith and mak my wame ful sklender,   *break; stomach; thin*
Quhilk usit wes before to meitis tender.'

'Weil, weil, sister,' quod the rurall mous,
'Geve it yow pleis, sic thing as ye se heir,   *if; please; such; here*
Baith meit and dreink, harberie and hous,   *lodging*
Sal be your awin, will ye remane al yeir.
Ye sall it have wyth blyith and mery cheir,   *happy*
And that suld mak the maissis that ar rude,   *dishes; rustic*
Amang freindis, richt tender, sueit, and gude.   *extremely*

'Quhat plesans is in feistis delicate,   *dainty feasts*
The quhilkis ar gevin with ane glowmand brow?   *which are given; frowning*
Ane gentill hart is better recreate   *noble; refreshed*
With blyith visage, than seith to him ane kow.
Ane modicum is mair for till allow,   *to praise*
Swa that gude will be kerver at the dais,   *provided that; carver; high table*
Than thrawin vult and mony spycit mais.'   *twisted face; many spiced dishes*

For all hir mery exhortatioun
This burges mous had littill will to sing,
Bot hevilie scho kest hir browis doun,   *sorrowfully; cast; eyebrows*
For all the daynteis that scho culd hir bring;
Yit at the last scho said, halff in hething,   *scorn*
'Sister, this victuall and your royall feist   *food*
May weill suffice unto ane rurall beist.

'Lat be this hole and cum unto my place: *leave*
I sall to yow schaw, be experience,   *by*
My Gude Friday is better nor your Pace,   *Good Friday; Easter*
My dische likingis is worth your haill expence.   *whole expenditure*
I have housis anew off grit defence;
Off cat, na fall, na trap, I have na dreid.'   *mouse-trap*
'I grant,' quod scho, and on togidder thay yeid.   *went*

In skugry ay, throw rankest gers and corne,   *Secrecy; thickest grass*
Under cowert full prevelie couth thay creip;   *cover; stealthily; crept*
The eldest wes the gyde and went beforne,
The younger to hir wayis tuke gude keip.
On nicht thay ran and on the day can sleip,
Quhill in the morning, or the laverok sang,
Thay fand the town, and in blythlie couth gang.

Not fer fra thyne, unto ane worthie vane,   *dwelling*
This burges brocht thame sone quhare thay suld be.   *quickly*
Withowt God speid thair herberie wes tane   *lodging*
In to ane spence with vittell grit plentie: *pantry; food in abundance*
Baith cheis and butter upon skelfis hie,   *high shelves*
And flesche and fische aneuch, baith fresche and salt,
And sekkis full off grotis, meill, and malt.   *sack; oats; meal*

Efter, quhen thay disposit wer to dyne,
Withowtin grace, thay wesche and went to meit,   *washed; food*
With all coursis that cukis culd devyne,   *cooks; devise*
Muttoun and beif, strikin in tailyeis greit.   *carved in big slices*
Ane lordis fair thus couth thay counterfeit   *imitated*
Except ane thing: thay drank the watter cleir
In steid off wyne; bot yit thay maid gude cheir.

With blyith upcast, and merie countenance,
The eldest sister sperit at hir gest   *asked; guest*
Giff that scho be ressone fand difference
Betuix that chalmer and hir sarie nest.   *wretched*
'Ye, dame,' quod scho, 'bot how lang will this lest?'   *yes*
'For evermair, I wait, and langer to.'   *expect*
'Giff it be swa, ye ar at eis,' quod scho.   *so; in comfort*

Till eik thair cheir ane subcharge furth scho brocht,
Ane plait off grottis and ane disch full off meill;   *plate of oats*
Thraf caikkis als I trow scho spairit nocht   *oatcakes; believe; did not spare*
Aboundantlie about hir for to deill,   *serve*
And mane full fyne scho brocht in steid off geill,   *white bread; jelly*
And ane quhyte candill owt off ane coffer stall   *white candle; chest; stole*
In steid off spyce, to gust thair mouth withall.

This maid thay merie, quhill thay micht na mair,   *until they could no more*
And 'Haill, Yule, haill!' cryit upon hie.   *loudly*
Yit efter joy oftymes cummis cair,   *often comes sorrow*
And troubill efter grit prosperitie.
Thus as thay sat in all thair jolitie,
The spenser come with keyis in his hand,   *steward come*
Oppinnit the dure, and thame at denner fand.   *opened the door; found*

[116]

They taryit not to wesche, as I suppose,   *did not wait to wash*
Bot on to ga, that micht formest win.   *off they went*
The burges had ane hole, and in scho gois;
Hir sister had na hole to hyde hir in.
To se that selie mous, it wes grit sin;   *wretched; pity*
So desolate and will off ane gude reid;   *bewildered plan*
For verray dreid scho fell in swoun neir deid.   *sheer; almost dead*

Bot, as God wald, it fell ane happie cace: *willed*
The spenser had na laser for to byde,   *leisure; stay*
Nowther to seik nor serche, to char nor chace,   *frighten nor chase*
Bot on he went, and left the dure up wyde.   *door; open wide*
The bald burges his passing weill hes spyde;   *bold*
Out off hir hole scho come and cryit on hie,
'How fair ye, sister? Cry peip, quhair ever ye be!'

This rurall mous lay flatling on the ground,   *flat*
And for the deith scho wes full sair dredand,   *was sorely fearing death*
For till hir hart straik mony wofull stound;   *to her heart struck; pang*
As in ane fever trimbillit fute and hand;   *trembled; foot*
And quhan hir sister in sic ply hir fand,   *when; plight*
For verray pietie scho began to greit,   *pity; cry*
Syne confort hir with wordis hunny sweit.   *comforted; sweet as honey*

'Quhy ly ye thus? Ryse up, my sister deir!
Cum to your meit; this perrell is overpast.'
The uther answerit hir with hevie cheir,   *sorrowfully*
'I may not eit, sa sair I am agast.   *eat*
I had lever thir fourty dayis fast   *rather; these*
With watter caill, and to gnaw benis or peis,   *cabbage soup*
Than all your feist in this dreid and diseis.'   *distress*

With fair tretie yit scho gart hir upryse,   *entreaty; caused her to get up*
And to the burde thay went and togidder sat.   *table; together*
And scantlie had thay drunkin anis or twyse,   *scarcely; once*
Quhen in come Gib Hunter, our jolie cat,
And bad 'God speid'. The burges up with that,   *'Good day'; leapt up*
And till hir hole scho fled as fyre of flint;   *fire from a flint*
Bawdronis the uther be the bak hes hint.   *[Scottish name for a cat]; seized*

Fra fute to fute he kest hir to and fra,   *tossed*
Quhylis up, quhylis doun, als tait as ony kid.   *brisk; child*
Quhylis wald he lat hir rin under the stra;   *run; straw*
Quhylis wald he wink, and play with hir buk heid;   *blindman's buff*
Thus to the selie mous grit pane he did;
Quhill at the last throw fortune and gude hap,   *good luck*
Betwix the dosor and the wall scho crap.   *wall hanging; crept*

And up in haist behind the parraling   *tapestry*
Scho clam so hie that Gilbert micht not get hir,   *climbed*
Syne be the cluke thair craftelie can hing   *claw; hung there*
Till he wes gane; hir cheir wes all the better.   *gone; spirit*
Syne doun scho lap quhen thair wes nane to let hir,   *leapt; hinder*
Apon the burges mous loud can scho cry,   *did*
'Fairweill, sister, thy feist heir I defy!   *renounce*

'Thy mangerie is mingit all with cair;   *banquet; mixed*
Thy guse is gude, thy gansell sour as gall;
The subcharge off thy service is bot sair;   *extra course; only sorrow*
Sa sall thow find heir-efterwart may fall.   *hereafter*
I thank yone courtyne and yone perpall wall   *curtain; partition*
Off my defence now fra yone crewell beist.
Almichtie God keip me fra sic ane feist.   *keep*

[118]

'Wer I into the kith that I come fra,
For weill nor wo suld I never cum agane.'
With that scho tuke hir leif and furth can ga,   *leave; went off*
Quhylis throw the corne and quhylis throw the plane.   *plain*
Quhen scho wes furth and fre scho wes full fane,   *away; glad*
And merilie markit unto the mure;   *went*
I can not tell how eftirwart scho fure,   *fared*

Bot I hard say scho passit to hir den,
Als warme as woll, suppose it wes not greit,   *wool; even though; big*
Full beinly stuffit, baith but and ben,
Off beinis and nuttis, peis, ry, and quheit;   *wheat*
Quhen ever scho list scho had aneuch to eit,   *whenever; wished; enough*
In quyet and eis withoutin ony dreid,
Bot to hir sisteris feist na mair scho yeid.   *went*

Moralitas

Freindis, heir may ye find, and ye will tak heid,
In this fabill ane gude moralitie:
As fitchis myngit ar with nobill seid,   *mixed weeds; seed*
Swa interminglit is adversitie   *intermixed*
With eirdlie joy, swa that na state is frie   *earthly; rank; free*
Without trubill and sum vexatioun,   *trouble*
And namelie thay quhilk clymmis up maist hie,   *those who climb; most*
That ar not content with small possessioun.   *possessions*

Blissed be sempill lyfe withoutin dreid;   *blessed*
Blissed be sober feist in quietie.   *moderate; quietness*
Quha hes aneuch, of na mair hes he neid,   *whoever*
Thocht it be littill into quantatie.   *though*

[119]

Grit aboundance and blind prosperitie
Oftymes makis ane evill conclusioun.
The sweitest lyfe, thairfoir, in this cuntrie,
Is sickernes, with small possessioun.   *security*

O wantoun man, that usis for to feid   *wanton; is accustomed*
Thy wambe and makis it a god to be,   *belly*
Luke to thy self, I warne the weill on deid.   *without doubt*
The cat cummis and to the mous hes ee;   *eye*
Quhat vaillis than thy feist and royaltie,   *avails*
With dreidfull hart and tribulatioun?
Thairfoir, best thing in eird, I say for me,   *earth*
Is merry hart with small possessioun.   *happiness*

Thy awin fyre, my freind, sa it be bot ane gleid,   *own; even if; ember*
It warmis weill, and is worth gold to the;   *thee*
And Solomon sayis, gif that thow will reid,   *read*
'Under the hevin thair can not better be
Than ay be blyith and leif in honestie.'   *ever; live*
Quhairfoir I may conclude be this ressoun: *wherefore; statement*
Of eirthly joy it beiris maist degré,   *holds the highest place*
Blyithnes in hart, with small possessioun.

ROBERT HENRYSON

The principal persecutor of the mouse is the cat: Tom and Jerry is an ancient story. Cat poems, though, dwell on other aspects of the feline condition, many of them written in frank admiration of the sheer talent that cats manifest in simply being themselves, no matter what we expect of them. One of my favourite cat poems is also one of the oldest, 'Pangur Bán', written by an Irish monk in the ninth century. The pursuit of mice comes into this poem – it being the counterpart of the poet's pursuit of knowledge. Then there is Christopher Smart's moving 'For I Will Consider my Cat Jeoffry', written in an asylum and a paean to a cat and his abilities. This poem contains a line to which all cat lovers will readily assent: 'For every house is incomplete without him and a blessing is lacking in the spirit.'

But, not so fast. Cats are not heroes. Cats are not loyal, as dogs are. Altruistic acts by cats are rare to non-existent. Don't rely on a cat to save you from anything.

Alastair Reid was accomplished and cosmopolitan. The range of his work is considerable, and includes translations of Neruda and Borges. In his *Weathering*, published in Edinburgh in 1978, he includes a poem 'Propinquity', which lays bare the selfishness of cats and their rootless, enigmatic existence. 'O folly, folly, / to love a cat,' says Reid. Anyone who has been suddenly deserted by a cat who has found a better home somewhere else will know what Reid means.

Propinquity

is the province of cats. Living by accident,
lapping the food at hand or sleeking down
in an adjacent lap when sleep occurs to them,
never aspiring to consistency
in homes or partners, unaware of property,
cats take their chances, love by need or nearness
as long as the need lasts, as long as the nearness
is near enough. The code of cats is simply
to take what comes. And those poor souls who claim
to own a cat, who long to recognise
in bland and narrowing eyes a look like love,
are bound to suffer should they expect
cats to come purring punctually home.
Home is only where the food and the fire are,
but might be anywhere. Cats fall on their feet,
nurse their own wounds, attend to their own laundry,
and purr at appropriate times. O folly, folly,
to love a cat, and yet
we dress with love the distance that they keep,
the hair-raising way they have, and easily blame
all their abandoned litters and torn ears
on some marauding tiger, well aware
that cats themselves do not care.

Yet part of us is cat. Confess –
love turns on accident and needs
nearness; and the various selves we have

accrue from our cat-wanderings, our chance
crossings. Imagination prowls at night,
cat-like, among odd possibilities.
Only our dog-sense brings us faithfully home,
makes meaning out of accident, keeps faith,
and, cat-and-dog, the arguments go at it.
But every night, outside, cat-voices call
us out to take a chance, to leave
the safety of our baskets and to let
what happens happen. 'Live, live!' they catcall.
'Each moment is your next! Propinquity,
Propinquity is all!

ALASTAIR REID

Sir Alexander Gray's 'On a Cat, Ageing' could be as much about people as it is about cats. We all want the equivalent of 'warmth and the glad procession / Of fish and milk and fish' but we all similarly notice the limitations that the years bring, even if forty is the new thirty, thirty the new twenty, and so on.

And here too are some poems about very different creatures: wild geese, a toad, and a basking shark, as well as a mole and of course the raven.

On a Cat, Ageing

He blinks upon the hearth-rug,
    And yawns in deep content,
Accepting all the comforts
    That Providence has sent.

Louder he purrs and louder,
    In one glad hymn of praise
For all the night's adventures,
    For quiet restful days.

Life will go on for ever,
    With all that cat can wish;
Warmth and the glad procession
    Of fish and milk and fish.

Only – the thought disturbs him –
   He's noticed once or twice,
The times are somehow breeding
   A nimbler race of mice.

SIR ALEXANDER GRAY

The Wild Geese

'Oh tell me what was on yer road, ye roarin' norlan' Wind,
As ye cam' blawin' frae the land that's niver frae my mind?
My feet they traivel England, but I'm deein' for the north.'
'My man, I heard the siller tides rin up the Firth o Forth.'

'Aye, Wind, I ken them weel eneuch, and fine they fa' and rise,
And fain I'd feel the creepin' mist on yonder shore that lies,
But tell me, ere ye passed them by, what saw ye on the way?'
'My man, I rocked the rovin' gulls that sail abune the Tay.'

'But saw ye naething, leein' Wind, afore ye cam' to Fife?
There's muckle lyin' 'yont the Tay that's mair to me nor life.'
'My man, I swept the Angus braes ye hae'na trod for years.'
'O Wind, forgi'e a hameless loon that canna see for tears!'

'And far abune the Angus straths I saw the wild geese flee,
A lang, lang skein o' beatin' wings, wi' their heids towards the sea,
And aye their cryin' voices trailed ahint them on the air –'
'O Wind, hae maircy, haud yer whisht, for I daurna listen mair!'

VIOLET JACOB

Toad

Stop looking like a purse. How could a purse
squeeze under the rickety door and sit,
full of satisfaction, in a man's house?

You clamber towards me on your four corners –
right hand, left foot, left hand, right foot.

I love you for being a toad,
for crawling like a Japanese wrestler,
and for not being frightened.

I put you in my purse hand, not shutting it,
and set you down outside directly under
every star.

A jewel in your head? Toad,
you've put one in mine,
a tiny radiance in a dark place.

NORMAN MacCAIG

Basking shark

To stub an oar on a rock where none should be,
To have it rise with a slounge out of the sea
Is a thing that happened once (too often) to me.

But not too often – though enough. I count as gain
That once I met, on a sea tin-tacked with rain,
That roomsized monster with a matchbox brain.

He displaced more than water. He shoggled me
Centuries back – this decadent townee
Shook on a wrong branch of his family tree.

Swish up the dirt and, when it settles, a spring
Is all the clearer. I saw me, in one fling,
Emerging from the slime of everything.

So who's the monster? The thought made me grow pale
For twenty seconds while, sail after sail,
The tall fin slid away and then the tail.

NORMAN MacCAIG

The Twa Corbies

As I was walking all alane,
I heard twa corbies makin a mane;   *moan*
The tane unto the t'other say,   *the one*
'Where sall we gang and dine to-day?'

'In behint yon auld fail dyke,   *turf wall*
I wot there lies a new slain knight;
And naebody kens that he lies there,
But his hawk, his hound an his lady fair.'

'His hound is tae the huntin gane,
His hawk tae fetch the wild-fowl hame,
His lady's ta'en another mate,
So we may mak oor dinner sweet.

'Ye'll sit on his white hause-bane,   *neck bone*
And I'll pike out his bonny blue een;   *eyes*
Wi' ae lock o' his gowden hair   *golden*
We'll theek oor nest when it grows bare.'   *thatch*

'Mony a one for him makes mane,
But nane sall ken whar he is gane;   *shall know*
O'er his white banes, when they are bare,
The wind sall blaw for evermair.'

ANON

Molecatcher

Strampin' the bent, like the Angel o' Daith
  The mowdie-man staves by;
Alang his pad the mowdie-worps
  Like sma' Assyrians lie.

And where the Angel o' Daith has been,
  Yirked oot o' their yirdy hames,
Lie Sennacherib's blasted hosts
  Wi' guts dung oot o' wames.

Sma' black tramorts wi' gruntles grey,
  Sma' weak weemin's han's,
Sma' bead-een that wid touch ilk hert
  Binnaae the mowdie-man's.

ALBERT MACKIE

There has been a recent revival of interest in the work of the Aberdonian writer Nan Shepherd. This has led to her enjoying the distinction of being the first woman to feature on a Royal Bank of Scotland banknote. Her classic work, *The Living Mountain*, places her in the front rank of Scottish nature writers. Mountains, in particular, move those who venture upon them or even see them from afar. Being on a mountain is, for some, a quasi-religious experience. As I write this, in Argyll, I look out from my window to the mountain only a short distance away. Rain falls in shifting veils; a waterfall, tripping over the rim of a high ridge, cascades down the mountainside to become the burn from which we draw out water for the house. Sometimes very low cloud, stratus fractus, creates a moving white line halfway up the hillside.

The Hill Burns

So without sediment
Run the clear burns of my country,
Fiercely pure,
Transparent as light
Gathered into its own unity,
Lucent and without colour;
Or green,
Like clear deeps of air,
Light massed upon itself,
Like the green pinions,
Cleaving the trouble of approaching night,
Shining in their own lucency,
Of the great angels that guarded the Mountain;

Or amber so clear
It might have oozed from the crystal trunk
Of the tree Paradisal,
Symbol of life,
That grows in the presence of God eternally.
And these pure waters
Leap from the adamantine rocks,
The granites and schists
Of my dark and stubborn country.
From gaunt heights they tumble,
Harsh and desolate lands,
The plateau of Braeriach
Where even in July
The cataracts of wind
Crash in the corries with the boom of seas in anger;
And Corrie Etchachan
Down whose precipitous
Narrow defile
Thunder the fragments of rock
Broken by winter storms
From their aboriginal place;
And Muich Dhui's summit,
Rock defiant against frost and the old grinding of ice,
Wet with the cold fury of blinding cloud,
Through which the snow-fields loom up, like ghosts from a
    world of eternal annihilation,
And far below, where the dark waters of Etchachan are
    wont to glint,
An unfathomable void.
Out of these mountains,

Out of the defiant torment of Plutonic rock,
Out of fire, terror, blackness and upheaval,
Leap the clear burns,
Living water,
Like some pure essence of being,
Invisible in itself,
Seen only by its movement.

NAN SHEPHERD

Loch Avon

Loch A'an, Loch A'an, hoo deep ye lie!
Tell nane yer depth and nane shall I.
Bricht though yer deepmaist pit may be,
Ye'll haunt me till the day I dee.
Bricht, an' bricht, an' bricht as air,
Ye'll haunt me noo for evermair.

NAN SHEPHERD

Summit of Corrie Etchachan

But in the climbing ecstasy of thought,
Ere consummation, ere the final peak,
Come hours like this. Behind, the long defile,
The steep rock-path, alongside which, from under
Snow-caves, sharp-corniced, tumble the ice-cold waters.
And now, here, at the corrie's summit, no peak,
No vision of the blue world, far, unattainable,
But this grey plateau, rock-strewn, vast, silent,
The dark loch, the toiling crags, the snow;
A mountain shut within itself, yet a world,
Immensity. So may the mind achieve,
Toiling, no vision of the infinite,
But a vast, dark and inscrutable sense
Of its own terror, its own glory and power.

NAN SHEPHERD

Birth, Joy, Life

We welcome new children with small ceremonies – the crossing of the palm with silver, the touching of the forehead, the giving of a kiss, the sprinkling of the head with water. We think of what lies ahead, and wish the child safe passage. We do not mention our anxieties, our doubts, as to the future of mankind and of this dear green planet. It's over to you, now. May our manifold and manifest mistakes not make your life's journey an impossible one.

Among such poems of bon voyage, George Mackay Brown's 'A New Child' is without equal. It is one of the most beautiful Scottish poems of the twentieth century. A close second, in my view, is 'Soave sia il vento', from Mozart's *Così fan Tutte*, where those departing are wished gentle winds to carry them on their journey. And of course there is Auden's 'Many Happy Returns', which is a birthday poem for a seven-year-old boy and one that wishes him balance in his life – a life that marries intellect and the senses, and which gives him that most sensible of advice – to follow his nose.

A New Child: ECL

I

Wait a while, small voyager
    On the shore, with seapinks and shells.

The boat
    Will take a few summers to build.
That you must make your voyage in.

II

You will learn the names.
That golden light is 'sun' – 'moon'
    The silver light
That grows and dwindles.

And the beautiful small splinters
    That wet the stones, 'rain'.

III

There is a voyage to make,
    A chart to read,
But not yet, not yet.
    'Daisies' spill from your fingers.
    The night daisies are 'stars'.

IV

The keel is laid, the strakes
    Will be set, in time.
A tree is growing
    That will be a tall mast

All about you, meantime
The music of humanity,
    The dance of creation:
Scored on the chart of the voyage.

V

The stories, legends, poems
Will be woven to make your sail.

You may hear the beautiful tale of Magnus
    Who took salt on his lip.
Your good angel
    Will be with you on that shore.

VI

Soon the voyage of EMMA
    To Tir-Nan-Og and beyond.

VII

Star of the Sea, shine on her voyage.

GEORGE MACKAY BROWN

How we feel about children is evident in almost every line of the poems that follow. This is one of the deepest of human feelings, experienced for the first time in the delivery room and then persisting for the rest of one's life. I remember how I felt when my first child was handed to me by the nurse, how I wept and how my daughter looked up at me and blinked at the light; in such surroundings and in such a way starts a love that lasts a lifetime. And was repeated, as an immense bonus, a second time. In Africa, a common name for a child is Gift, which recognises this so succinctly and charmingly. Another popular name in Africa is Precious, a wonderful name that must reassure the bearer that whatever happens in life, she was once, and may still be, of inestimable value to a doting parent.

To the Future

He, the unborn, shall bring
From blood and brain
Songs that a child can sing
And common men:

Songs that the heart can share
And understand;
Simple as berries are
Within the hand:

Such a sure simpleness
As strength may have;
Sunlight upon the grass:
The curve of the wave.

WILLIAM SOUTAR

Lily of Raasay

Lily of Raasay
gentle your growing
child of the islands
woodland and moor;
you will imagine
worlds for exploring
as you are stepping
over the shore.

Father and mother
comfort and hold you
their love is for you
better than gold.
Grant you courageous
sensible kindly
bonny and thoughtful
honest and bold.

Dark as the raven
eyes of the ocean
hazel and willow
wisdom and grace;
mountain and birchtrees
above and around you
light of the islands
shines from your face.

Lily of Raasay
what can I more say?
Now I behold you
give you my words.
When I have left here
they will be with you
silently singing
for all my sweet loves.

From Tessa with love for Lily in the month of May 2003

(Inspired by the tune of the carol 'Child in a Manger'. originally
written as 'Leonabh an Aigh' by Mary Macdonald of Bunessan;
Lily's great-grandfather was Minister of the parish of Bunessan.)

TESSA RANSFORD

For My Newborn Son

Blythe was yir comin,   *glad*
Hert never dreamt it,
A new man bidan   *staying*
In warld whan I've left it.

Bricht was yon morn,
Cauld in September,
Wi sun aa the causey   *street*
Glentered wi glamer,   *shone like magic*
Sclate roofs lik siller
Schire-bleezan yon morn.   *bright blazing*

Hert in my kist lap,   *chest*
Joyrife its dirlan,   *joyous; thumping*
Bairn, whan oor lips met
Yir mither's were burnan,
Weet were oor een then,
Puir words downa tell it.

As hert never dreamt on
Was joy in yir comin,
Maikless wee nesslin   *peerless*
Ma sleepan reid Robin.

SYDNEY GOODSIR SMITH

At First, My Daughter

She is world without understanding.
She is made of sound.
She drinks me.

We laugh when I lift her by the feet.
She is new as a petal.
Water comes out of her mouth and her little crotch.

She gives the crook of my arm
A weight of delight.
I stare in her moving mirror of untouched flesh.

Absurd, but verifiable,
These words – mother, daughter –
They taste of receiving and relinquishing.

She will never again be quite so novel and lovely
Nor I so astonished.
In touch, we are celebrating

The first and last moments
Of being together and separate
Indissolute – till we are split

By time, and growth, and man,
The things I made her with.

ELMA MITCHELL

Mother, Dear Mother

She is invigilator; her name is knife.
She changes nappies and sleeps in my father's bed.

If I cry blazes or trickle, she'll come to my whistle
And give me her breast. Or let me lie and cry.

Half of her's mine, and half is my hot fat father's.
To each, one arm, one eye – and then what?

What is the good of possessing half a woman?
I'll pull her down to me by her swinging hair

And eat her all up, moon-face, belly and toes,
And throw the skin to my father, to keep him warm.

ELMA MITCHELL

Invocation

Child in the little boat
Come to the land
Child of the seals
Calf of the whale
Spawn of the octopus
Fledgeling of cormorant
Gannet and herring-gull,
Come from the sea,
Child of the sun,
Son of the sky.
Safely pass
The mouths of the water,
The mouths of night,
The teeth of the rocks,
The mouths of the wind,
Safely float
On the dangerous waves
Of an ocean sounding
Deeper than red.
Darker than violet,
Safely cross
The ground-swell of pain
Of the waves that break
On the shores of the world.
Life everlasting
Love has prepared
The paths of your coming.

Plankton and nekton
Free-swimming pelagic
Spawn of the waters
Has brought you to birth
In the life-giving pools,
Spring has led you
Over the meadows
In fox's fur
Has nestled and warmed you,
With the houseless hare
In the rushes has sheltered,
Warm under feathers
Of brooding wings
Safe has hidden
In the grass secretly
Clothed in disguise
Of beetle and grasshopper
Small has laid you
Under a stone
In the nest of the ants
Myriadfold scattered
In pollen of pine forests
Set you afloat
Like dust on the air
And winged in multitudes
Hatched by the sun
From the mud of rivers.
Newborn you have lain
In the arms of mothers,
You have drawn life

From a myriad breasts,
The mating of animals
Has not appalled you,
The longing of lovers
You have not betrayed,
You have come unscathed
From the field of battle
From famine and plague
You have lived undefiled
In the gutters of cities
We have seen you dancing
Barefoot in villages,
You have been to school
But kept your wisdom.

Child in the little boat,
Come to the land,
Child of the seals.

KATHLEEN RAINE

Daedalus

My son has birds in his head.

I know them now. I catch
the pitch of their calls, their shrill
cacophonies, their chitterings, their coos.
They hover behind his eyes and come to rest
on a branch, on a book, grow still,
claws curled, wings furled.
He is a bird world.

I learn the flutter of his moods,
his moments of swoop and soar.
From the ground I feel him try
the limits of the air –
sudden lift, sudden terror –
and move in time to cradle
his quivering, feathered fear.

At evening, in the tower,
I see him to sleep and see
the hooding-over of eyes,
the slow folding of wings.
I wake to his morning twitterings,
to the *croomb* of his becoming.

He chooses his selves – wren, hawk,
swallow or owl – to explore
the trees and rooftops of his heady wishing.
Tomtit, birdie.
Am I to call him down, to give him
a grounding, teach him gravity?
Gently, gently.
Time tells us what we weigh, and soon enough
his feet will reach the ground.
Age, like a cage, will enclose him.
So the wise man said.

My son has birds in his head.

ALASTAIR REID

from A Bard's Address to His Youngest
   Daughter

Come to my arms my wee wee pet
My mild my blithesome Harriet
The sweetest babe art thou to me
That ever sat on parent's knee.
Thou hast that eye was mine erewhile
Thy mother's blithe and grateful smile
And such a playful merry vein
That greybeards smile at pranks of thine

And if aright I read thy mind
The child of nature thou'rt designed
For even while yet upon the breast
Thou mimic'st child and bird and beast
Can'st cry like Moggy o'er her book
And crow like cock and caw like rook
Boo like a bull and blare like ram
And bark like dog and bleat like lamb
And when abroad in pleasant weather
Thou mingiest all these sounds together
Then who can say, thou happy creature,
Thou'rt not the very child of nature

*

How dar'st thou frown, thou freakish fay,
And pout and look the other way?
Why turn thy chubby cheeks athraw
And skelp the beard of thy papa?
I know full well thy deep design
'Tis to turn back thine eye on mine
With triple burst of joyful glee
And fifty strains at mimicry
What wealth from nature may'st thou won
With pupilage so soon begun.
Well, hope is all; thou art unproved,
The bard's and nature's best beloved.
And now above thy brow so fair
And flowing films of flaxen hair
I lay my hand once more and frame
A blessing in the holy name
Of that supreme divinity
Who breathed a living soul in thee.

JAMES HOGG

Personal History

for my son

O my heart is the unlucky heir of the ages
And my body is unwillingly the secret agent
Of my ancestors; those content with their wages
From history: the Cumberland Quaker whose gentle
Face was framed with lank hair to hide the ears
Cropped as a punishment for this steadfast faith,
The Spanish lady who had seen the pitch lake's broth
In the West Indian island and the Fife farmers
To whom the felted barley meant a winter's want.

My face presents my history, and its sallow skin
Is parchment for the Edinburgh lawyer's deed:
To have and hold in trust, as feoffee therein
Until such date as the owner shall have need
Thereof. My brown eyes are jewels I cannot pawn,
And my long lip once curled beside an Irish bog,
My son's whorled ear was once my father's, then mine;
I am the map of a campaign, each ancestor has his flag
Marking an advance or a retreat. I am their seed.

As I write I look at the five fingers of my hand,
Each with its core of nacre bone, and rippled nails;
Turn to the palm and the traced unequal lines that end
In death – only at the tips my ancestry fails –
The dotted swirls are original and are my own:
Look at this fringed polyp which I daily use

And ask its history, ask to what grave abuse
It has been put: perhaps it curled about the stone
Of Cain. At least it has known much of evil,

And perhaps as much of good, been tender
When tenderness was needed, and been firm
On occasion, and in its past been free of gender,
Been the hand of a mother holding the warm
Impress of the child against her throbbing breast,
Been cool to the head inflamed in fever,
Sweet and direct in contact with a lover.
O in its cupped and fluted shell lies all the past;
My fingers close about the crash of history's storm.

In the tent of night I hear the voice of Calvin
Expending his hatred of the world in icy words;
Man less than a red ant beneath the towering mountain,
And God a troll more fearful than the feudal lords;
The Huguenots in me, flying Saint Bartholomew's Day,
Are in agreement with all this, and their resentful hate
Flames brighter than the candles on an altar, the grey
Afternoon is lit by Catherine Wheels of terror, the street
Drinks blood and pity is death before their swords.

The cantilever of my bones acknowledges the architect,
My father, to whom always the world was a mystery
Concealed in the humped base of a bottle, one solid fact
To set against the curled pages and the tears of history.
I am a Border keep, a croft and a solicitor's office,
A country rectory, a farm and a drawing-board:

In me, as in so many, the past has stored its miser's hoard,
Won who knows where nor with what loaded dice.
When my blood pulses it is their blood I feel hurry.

These forged me, the latest link in a fertile chain
With ends that run so far that my short sight
Cannot follow them, nor can my weak memory claim
Acquaintance with the earliest shackle. In my height
And breadth I hold my history, and then my son
Holds my history in his small body and the history of another,
Who for me has no contact but that of flesh, his mother.
What I make now I make, indeed, from the unknown,
A blind man spinning furiously in the web of night.

RUTHVEN TODD

War, Conflict & Loss

The poems in this section are all about loss and the feelings that loss evokes. Life is a series of losses, if one comes to think of it: the loss of the security and comfort of childhood, the loss of innocence, the loss of friends as one goes off to study or earn a living, and then all the later losses that seem to speed up as you go through life. That sounds like a bleak picture, and it would be, I suppose, if there were not so much else to life – so many positive experiences and delights. Ultimately one has to decide which side of the ledger – positive or negative – is going to dominate one's view of the world, and that, as more than one school of philosophy has proposed, is one of life's great questions.

Death, of course, is the greatest loss – for the person who dies, and for those left behind. Norman MacCaig's 'Memorial' is a haunting poem about how the death of one person persists in the life of a survivor – who becomes the dead person's 'sad music'. Death may haunt those left behind, but that was not always so in times when there was utter confidence that death was a beginning as well as an end. George Buchanan, the sixteenth-century humanist scholar and poet, would have believed implicitly in the survival of the human soul. Buchanan, who was tutor to the young James VI – whom he bullied into a love of literature – wrote a poem on the death of the great theologian, Jean Calvin. 'Elegy on Jean Calvin' is an example of confidence in the future beyond the grave – one which takes the dead person 'beyond the stars'. There is no room for doubt in Buchanan's lines – something that would be impossible today in any poetic discussion of what happens to us when we die.

Hamish Henderson's 'Flyting o' Lif and Daith' is a dialogue between life and death, with life having the last word on the matter. In this poem there are shining paeans to the affirmation of life in the face of death's claim. I particularly like this:

Quo life, the warld is mine.
Your deadly wark, I ken it fine.
There's maet on earth for ilka wean.
Quo life, the warld is mine.

'There's maet on earth for ilka wean . . .' In that beautiful line, Hamish Henderson, a man of great sympathy and feeling for those whose life is blighted by poverty or oppression, says what surely has to be said to those who turn their faces against the needs of the weak and humble. This single line could be a powerful motto for any charity working to alleviate suffering amongst children who have to fend for themselves on a rubbish dump somewhere, or who are exploited in debt bondage or slavery, or who simply do not get their fair share.

'The Flyting o' Lif and Daith' is followed by several other poems, drawn from Hamish Henderson's body of work. These are some of the finest war poetry ever written in Scotland or by a Scottish poet. I remember hearing Hamish singing one of these poems – it is usually sung – in a room in George Square in Edinburgh. He was a tall, rather ungainly man, a bit like a well-built scarecrow, and he often wore a hat that no self-respecting scarecrow would consider wearing. He smiled at people with a gentle, wise smile, exposing teeth that seemed to go in all sorts of directions. He had a gentle, good face. And there he was, sitting on a table rather than at it, singing, unaccompanied, that great poem he wrote, 'The 51st Highland Division's Farewell to Sicily'. That simple tune, so easy to remember and to hum or whistle, never leaves you once you have heard it. It breaks the heart. At the end of Hamish's singing, as I recall, there was silence. Each one of us, I think, felt that we had been in the presence of something very significant and for a few moments had been transported back to those eerie 'bricht chaulmers' only recently left by the Highlanders going north and into a great battle for civilization itself.

'Heroes', by Sorley MacLean, presented here both in the original Gaelic and English translation by the poet, is an example of the magnanimity that Scotland is well capable of but which can sometimes be drowned out by strident complaint and a chorus of orchestrated grievance. MacLean 'saw an Englishman in Egypt' whose death 'took a little weeping to my eyes'. This is a very moving poem because of its generosity of spirit. England and Scotland have often been on different sides in the past, but, as Hamish Henderson points out in *Elegies for the Dead in Cyrenaica*, hatred disfigures.

Memorial

Everywhere she dies. Everywhere I go she dies.
No sunrise, no city square, no lurking beautiful mountain
but has her death in it.
The silence of her dying sounds through
the carousel of language, it's a web
on which laughter stitches itself. How can my hand
clasp another's when between them
is that thick death, that intolerable distance?

She grieves for my grief. Dying, she tells me
that bird dives from the sun, that fish
leaps into it. No crocus is carved more gently
than the way her dying
shapes my mind. – But I hear, too,
the other words,
black words that make the sound
of soundlessness, that name the nowhere
she is continuously going into.

Ever since she died
she can't stop dying. She makes me
her elegy. I am a walking masterpiece,
a true fiction
of the ugliness of death.
I am her sad music.

NORMAN MacCAIG

from Elegy of Jean Calvin

For the dead weight of your body with its apprehensions
Has left you, you are beyond the stars, you nudge
God, you enjoy the one your mind adored,
You see pure light within pure light, you drink
Divinity poured brimming into you,
Your life has become an everlasting thing
Unanxious, impervious to empty-headed joys
Or devastating fears or the hammer of grief
Or the cancer of disease creeping from body to soul.
As for me, I call that morning which released you
From bitterest cares a very birthday: snatched
To the stars, you re-entered your old homeland,
You left a repellent exile behind, your mind
Scoffs at any second death, rules the supposed
Rule of fate, steps into the vista
Of an immeasurable life.

GEORGE BUCHANAN
translated by
EDWIN MORGAN

The Heart Could Never Speak

The heart could never speak
But that the Word was spoken.
We hear the heart break
Here with hearts unbroken.
Time teach us the art
That breaks and heals the heart.

Heart, you would be dumb
But that your word was said
In time, and the echoes come
Thronging from the dead.
Time, teach us the art
That resurrects the heart.

Tongue, you can only say
Syllables, joy and pain,
Till time, having its way,
Makes the word live again.
Time, merciful lord,
Grant us to learn your word.

EDWIN MUIR

Requiem

Under the wide and starry sky
Dig the grave and let me die.
Glad did I live and gladly die,
  And I laid me down with a will.

This be the verse you grave for me:
Here he lies where he longed to be;
Home is the sailor, home from the sea,
  And the hunter home from the hill.

ROBERT LOUIS STEVENSON

Flyting o' Lif and Daith

Quo life, the warld is mine.
The floo'ers and trees, they're a' my ain.
I am the day, and the sunshine.
Quo life, the warld is mine.

Quo daith, the warld is mine.
Your lugs are deef, your een are blin.
Your floo'ers maun dwine in my bitter win'.
Quo daith, the warld is mine.

Quo life, the warld is mine.
I hae saft win's, an' healin' rain.
Aipples I hae, an' breid an' wine.
Quo life, the warld is mine.

Quo daith, the warld is mine.
Whit sterts in dreid, gangs doon in pain.
Bairns wantin' breid are makin' mane.
Quo daith, the warld is mine.

Quo life, the warld is mine.
Your deadly wark, I ken it fine.
There's maet on earth for ilka wean.
Quo life, the warld is mine.

Quo daith, the warld is mine.
Your silly sheaves crine in my fire.
My worm keeks in your barn and byre.
Quo daith, the warld is mine.

Quo life, the warld is mine.
Dule on your een! Ae galliard hert
Can ban tae hell your blackest airt.
Quo life, the warld is mine.

Quo daith, the warld is mine.
Your rantin' hert, in duddies braw,
He winna lowp my preeson wa'.
Quo daith, the warld is mine.

Quo life, the warld is mine.
Thou ye bigg preesons o' marble stane
Hert's luve ye cannae preeson in.
Quo life, the warld is mine.

Quo daith, the warld is mine.
I hae dug a grave, I hae dug it deep,
For war an' the pest will gar ye sleep.
Quo death, the warld is mine.

Quo life, the warld is mine.
An open grave is a furrow syne.
Ye'll no keep my seed frae fa'in in.
Quo life, the warld is mine.

HAMISH HENDERSON

The 51st Highland Division's Farewell to Sicily

The pipie is dozie, the pipie is fey,
He winna come roon' for his vino the day.
The sky ow'r Messina is unco an' grey,
  An' a' the bricht chaulmers are eerie.

Then fare weel ye banks o' Sicily,
Fare ye weel ye valley and shaw.
There's nae Jock will mourn the kyles o' ye,
  Puir bliddy swaddies are wearie.

Fare weel, ye banks o' Sicily,
Fare ye weel, ye valley and shaw.
There's nae hame can smoor the wiles o' ye,
  Puir bliddy swaddies are wearie.

Then doon the stair and line the waterside,
Wait your turn, the ferry's awa'.
Then doon the stair and line the waterside,
  A' the bricht chaulmers are eerie.

The drummie is polisht, the drummie is braw
He cannae be seen for his webbin' ava.
He's beezed himsel' up for a photy an a'
  Tae leave wi' his Lola, his dearie.

Sae fare weel, ye dives o' Sicily
(Fare ye weel, ye shieling an' ha'),
We'll a' mind shebeens and bothies
  Whaur kind signorinas were cheerie.

Fare weel, ye banks o' Sicily
(Fare ye weel, ye shielings an' ha');
We'll a' mind shebeens and bothies
  Whaur Jock made a date wi' his dearie.

Then tune the pipes and drub the tenor drum
(Leave your kit this side o' the wa').
Then tune the pipes and drub the tenor drum
  A' the bricht chaulmers are eerie.

HAMISH HENDERSON

So Long

To the war in Africa that's over – goodnight.

To thousands of assorted vehicles, in every stage of
  decomposition
  littering the desert from here to Tunis – goodnight.

To thousands of guns and armoured fighting vehicles
  brewed up, blackened and charred
  from Alamein to here, from here to Tunis – goodnight.

To thousands of crosses of every shape and pattern,
  alone or in little huddles, under which the
    unlucky bastards lie –
      goodnight.

    Horse-shoe curve of the bay
    clean razor-edge of the escarpment,
  tonight it's the sunset only that's blooding you.

Halfaya and Sollum; I think that at long last
  we can promise you a little quiet.
So long, I hope I won't be seeing you.

To the sodding desert – you know what you
  can do with yourself.

To the African deadland – God help you –
and goodnight.

HAMISH HENDERSON

Seventh Elegy

Seven Good Germans

*The track running between Mekili and Tmimi was at one time a
kind of no-man's-land. British patrolling was energetic, and there
were numerous brushes with German and Italian elements. El Eleba
lies about halfway along this track.*

      Of the swaddies
      who came to the desert with Rommel
there were few who had heard (or would hear) of El Eleba.
They recce'd,
      or acted as medical orderlies
or patched up their tanks in the camouflaged workshops
and never gave a thought to a place like El Eleba.

To get there you drive into the blue, take a bearing
and head for damn-all. Then you're there. And where are
you?

– Still, of some few who did cross our path at El Eleba
there are seven who bide under their standing crosses.

The first a Lieutenant.
      When the medicos passed him

for service overseas, he had jotted in a note-book
to the day and the hour   keep me steadfast   there is only
the decision and the will
                    the rest has no importance

The second a Corporal.
                    He had been in the Legion
and had got one more chance to redeem his lost honour.
What he said was
Listen here, I'm fed up with your griping –
If you want extra rations, go get 'em from Tommy!
You're green, that's your trouble. Dodge the column, pass the buck
and scrounge all you can – that's our law in the Legion.
You know Tommy's got 'em . . . He's got mineral waters,
and beer, and fresh fruit in that white crinkly paper
and God knows what all! Well, what's holding you back?
Are you windy or what?
                    Christ, you 'old Afrikaners'!
If you're wanting the eats, go and get 'em from Tommy!

The third had been a farm-hand in the March of Silesia
and had come to the desert as fresh fodder for machine guns.
His dates are inscribed on the files, and on the crosspiece.

The fourth was a lance-jack.
                    He had trusted in Adolf
while working as a chemist in the suburb of Spandau.
His loves were his 'cello, and the woman who had borne
    him

two daughters and a son. He had faith in the Endsieg.
THAT THE NEW REICH MAY LIVE prayed the flyleaf
                                        of his Bible.

The fifth a mechanic.
                        All the honour and glory,
the siege of Tobruk and the conquest of Cairo
meant as much to that Boche as the Synod of Whitby.
Being wise to all this, he had one single headache.
which was, how to get back to his sweetheart (called Ilse).
– He had said

            Can't the Tommy wake up and get weaving?
If he tried, he could put our whole Corps in the bag. May
God damn this Libya and both of its palm-trees!

The sixth was a Pole
                        – or to you, a Volksdeutscher –
who had put off his nation to serve in the Wehrmacht.
He siegheiled, and talked of 'the dirty Polacken'.
and said what he'd do if let loose among Russkis.
His mates thought that, though 'just a polnischer
                                        Schweinhund'.
he was not a bad bloke.
                        On the morning concerned
he was driving a truck with mail, petrol and rations.
The M. P. on duty shouted five words of warning.
He nodded
            laughed
                        revved

and drove straight for El Eleba
not having quite got the chap's Styrian lingo.

The seventh a young swaddy.
Riding cramped in a lorry
to death along the road which winds eastward to Halfaya
he had written three verses in appeal against his sentence
which soften for an hour the anger of Lenin.

Seven poor bastards
dead in African deadland
(tawny tousled hair under the issue blanket)
wie einst Lili
dead in African deadland

einst Lili Marlene

HAMISH HENDERSON

On Looking at the Dead

This is a coming to reality.
This is the stubborn place. No metaphors swarm

around that fact, around that strangest thing,
that being that was and now no longer is.

This is a coming to a rock in space
worse than a rock (or less), diminished thing

worse and more empty than an empty vase.

The devious mind elaborates its rays.
This is the stubborn thing. It will not move.

It will not travel from our stony gaze.

But it must stay and that's the worst of it
till changed by processes. Otherwise it stays.

To beat against it and no waves of grace
ever to ascend or sovereign price

to be held above it! This is no hero. This
is an ordinary death. If there is grace

theology is distant. Sanctify
(or so they say) whatever really is

and this is real, nothing more real than this.
It beats you down to it, will not permit

the play of imagery, the peacock dance,
the bridal energy or mushrooming crown

or any blossom. It only is itself.
It isn't you. It only is itself.

It is the stubbornness of a real thing

mentionable as such and only such,
the eyes returning nothing. Compromise

is not a meaning of this universe.
And that is good. To face it where it is,

to stand against it in no middle way
but in the very centre where things are

and having it as centre, for you take
directions from it not as from a book

but from this star, black and fixed and here,
a brutal thing where no chimeras are

nor purple colours nor a gleam of silk
nor any embroideries eastern or the rest

but unavoidable beyond your choice
and therefore central and of major price.

IAIN CRICHTON SMITH

The Transmutation

That all should change to ghost and glance and gleam,
And so transmuted stand beyond all change,
And we be poised between the unmoving dream
And the sole moving moment – this is strange

Past all contrivance, word, or image, or sound,
Or silence, to express, that we who fall
Through time's long ruin should weave this phantom
    ground
And in its ghostly borders gather all.

There incorruptible the child plays still,
The lover waits beside the trysting tree,
The good hour spans its heaven, and the ill,
Rapt in their silent immortality,

As in commemoration of a day
That having been can never pass away.

EDWIN MUIR

The Brig

I whiles gang to the brig-side
That's past the briar tree,
Alang the road when the licht is wide
Ower Angus an the sea.
In by the dyke yon briar growes
Wi leaf an thorn, it's lane
Whaur the spunk o flame o the briar rose
Burns saft agin the stane.
An whiles a step treids on by me,
I mauna hear its fa';
An atween the brig an the briar tree
Ther gangs na ane, but twa.
Oot ower yon sea, throu duil an strife,
Ye tak yer road nae mair,
For ye've crossed the brig to the fields o life,
An ye walk for iver there.
I traivel on to the brig-side,
Whaur ilka road maun cease,
My weary war mey be lang to bide,
An you hae won to peace.
There's ne'er a nicht but turns to day,
Nor a load that's niver cast;
An there's nae wind cries on the winter brae,
But it spends itsel at last.
O you that flyer failed me yet,
Gin aince my step ye hear,
Come to yon brig atween us set,
An bide till I win near!

O weel, aye, weel, ye'll ken my treid,
Ye'll seek nae wird nor sign,
An I'll no can fail at the Brig o Dreid,
For yer hand will be in mine.

VIOLET JACOB

Departure and Departure and . . .

Someone is waving a white handkerchief
from the train as it pulls out with a white
plume from the station and rumbles its way
to somewhere that does not matter. But
it will pass the white sands and the broad sea
that I have watched under the sun and moon
in the stop of time in my childhood as I am
now there again and waiting for the white
handkerchief. I shall not see her again
but the waters rise and fall and the horizon
is firm. You who have not seen that line
hold the brimming sea to the round earth
cannot know this pain and sweetness of departure.

GEORGE BRUCE

At My Father's Grave

The sunlicht still on me, you row'd in clood,
We look upon each ither noo like hills,
Across a valley. I'm nae mair your son.
It is my mind, nae son o' yours, that looks,
And the great darkness o' your death comes up
And equals it across the way.
A livin' man upon a dead man thinks
And ony sma'er thocht's impossible.

HUGH MacDIARMID

The Horses

Barely a twelvemonth after
The seven days war that put the world to sleep,
Late in the evening the strange horses came.
By then we had made our covenant with silence,
But in the first few days it was so still
We listened to our breathing and were afraid.
On the second day
The radios failed; we turned the knobs, no answer.
On the third day a warship passed us, headed north,
Dead bodies piled on the deck. On the sixth day
A plane plunged over us into the sea. Thereafter
Nothing. The radios dumb;
And still they stand in corners of our kitchens,
And stand, perhaps, turned on, in a million rooms
All over the world. But now if they should speak,
If on a sudden they should speak again,
If on the stroke of noon a voice should speak,
We would not listen, we would not let it bring
That old bad world that swallowed its children quick
At one great gulp. We would not have it again.
Sometimes we think of the nations lying asleep,
Curled blindly in impenetrable sorrow,
And then the thought confounds us with its strangeness.

The tractors lie about our fields; at evening
They look like dank sea-monsters crouched and waiting.
We leave them where they are and let them rust:
'They'll molder away and be like other loam'.

We make our oxen drag our rusty ploughs,
Long laid aside. We have gone back
Far past our fathers' land.
                        And then, that evening
Late in the summer the strange horses came.
We heard a distant tapping on the road,
A deepening drumming; it stopped, went on again
And at the corner changed to hollow thunder.
We saw the heads
Like a wild wave charging and were afraid.
We had sold our horses in our fathers' time
To buy new tractors. Now they were strange to us
As fabulous steeds set on an ancient shield
Or illustrations in a book of knights.
We did not dare go near them. Yet they waited,
Stubborn and shy, as if they had been sent
By an old command to find our whereabouts
And that long-lost archaic companionship.
In the first moment we had never a thought
That they were creatures to be owned and used.
Among them were some half a dozen colts
Dropped in some wilderness of the broken world,
Yet new as if they had come from their own Eden.
Since then they have pulled our ploughs and borne our loads,
But that free servitude still can pierce our hearts.
Our life is changed; their coming our beginning.

EDWIN MUIR

From the Line

Have you seen men come from the Line,
Tottering, doddering, as if bad wine
Had drugged their very souls;
Their garments rent with holes
And caked with mud
And streaked with blood
Of others, or their own;
Haggard, weary-limbed and chilled to the bone,
Trudging aimless, hopeless, on
With listless eyes and faces drawn
Taut with woe?

Have you seen them aimless go
Bowed down with muddy pack
And muddy rifle slung on back,
And soaking overcoat,
Staring on with eyes that note
Nothing but the mire
Quenched of every fire?

Have you seen men when they come
From shell-holes filled with scum
Of mud and blood and flesh,
Where there's nothing fresh
Like grass, or trees, or flowers,
And the numbing year-like hours
Lag on – drag on,
And the hopeless dawn

Brings naught but death, and rain –
The rain a fiend of pain
That scourges without end,
And Death, a smiling friend?

Have you seen men when they come from hell?
If not, – ah, well
Speak not with easy eloquence
That seems like sense
Of 'War and its Necessity'!
And do not rant, I pray,
On 'War's Magnificent Nobility'!

If you've seen men come from the Line
You'll know it's Peace that is divine!
If you've not seen the things I've sung –
Let silence bind your tongue,
But, make all wars to cease,
And work, and work for Everlasting Peace!

RODERICK WATSON KERR

Curaidhean

Chan fhaca mi Lannes aig Ratasbon
no MacGillFhinnein aig Allt Èire
no Gill-Ìosa aig Cùil Lodair,
ach chunnaic mi Sasannach san Èipheit.

Fear beag truagh le gruaidhean pluiceach
is glùinean a' bleith a chèile,
aodann guireanach gun tlachd ann –
còmhdach an spioraid bu trèine.

Cha robh buaidh air 'san taigh-òsta
'n àm nan dòrn a bhith gan dùnadh',
ach leòmhann e ri uchd a' chatha,
anns na frasan guineach mùgach.

Thàinig uair-san leis na sligean,
leis na spealgan-iarainn beàrnach,
anns an toit is anns an lasair,
ann an crith is maoim na h-àraich.

Thàinig fios dha san fhrois pheilear
e bhith gu spreigearra 'na dhiùlnach:
is b' e sin e fhad 's a mhair e,
ach cha b' fhada fhuair e dh'ùine.

Chùm e ghunnachan ris na tancan,
a' bocail le sgreuch shracaidh stàirnich
gus an d' fhuair e fhèin mun stamaig

Heroes

I did not see Lannes at Ratisbon
nor MacLennan at Auldearn
nor Gillies MacBain at Culloden,
but I saw an Englishman in Egypt.

A poor little chap with chubby cheeks
and knees grinding each other,
pimply unattractive face –
garment of the bravest spirit.

He was not a hit 'in the pub
in the time of the fists being closed',
but a lion against the breast of battle,
in the morose wounding showers.

His hour came with the shells,
with the notched iron splinters,
in the smoke and flame,
in the shaking and terror of the battlefield.

Word came to him in the bullet shower
that he should be a hero briskly,
and he was that while he lasted,
but it wasn't much time he got.

He kept his guns to the tanks,
bucking with tearing crashing screech,
until he himself got, about the stomach,

an deannal ud a chuir ri làr e,
beul sìos an gainmhich 's an greabhal,
gun diog o ghuth caol grànda.

Cha do chuireadh crois no meadal
ri uchd no ainm no g' a chàirdean:
cha robh a bheag dhe f hòirne maireann,
's nan robh cha bhiodh am facal làidir;
's co-dhiù, ma sheasas ursann-chatha,
leagar mòran air a shàillibh
gun dùil ri cliù, nach iarr am meadal
no cop sam bith à beul na h-àraich.

Chunnaic mi gaisgeach mòr à Sasainn,
fearachan bochd nach laigheadh sùil air;
cha b' Alasdair à Gleanna Garadh –
is thug e gal beag air mo shùilean.

SOMHAIRLE MacGILL-EAIN

that biff that put him to the ground,
mouth down in sand and gravel,
without a chirp from his ugly high-pitched voice.

No cross or medal was put to his
chest or to his name or to his family;
there were not many of his troop alive,
and if there if there were their word would not be strong.
And at any rate, if a battle post stands,
many are knocked down because of him,
not expecting fame, not wanting a medal
or any froth from the mouth of the field of slaughter.

I saw a great warrior of England,
a poor manikin on whom no eye would rest;
no Alasdair of Glen Garry;
and he took a little weeping to my eyes.

SORLEY MacLEAN

Latha Foghair

'S mi air an t-slios ud
latha foghair,
na sligean a' sianail mum chluasan
agus sianar marbh ri mo ghualainn,
rag-mharbh – is reòthta mur b' e 'n teas –
mar gum b' ann a' fuireach ri fios.

Nuair thàinig an sgriach
a-mach às a' ghrèin,
à buille 's bualadh do-fhaicsinn,
leum an lasair agus streap an ceathach
agus bhàrc e gacha rathad:
dalladh nan sùl, sgoltadh claistinn.

'S 'na dhèidh, an sianar marbh,
fad an latha;
am measg nan sligean san t-srannraich
anns a' mhadainn,
agus a-rithist aig meadhan-latha
agus san fheasgar.

Ris a' ghrèin 's i cho coma,
cho geal cràiteach;
air a' ghainmhich 's i cho tìorail
socair bàidheil;
agus fo reultan Afraga,
's iad leugach àlainn.

An Autumn Day

On that slope
on an autumn day,
the shells soughing about my ears
and six dead men at my shoulder,
dead and stiff – and frozen were it not for the heat –
as if they were waiting for a message.

When the screech came
out of the sun,
out of an invisible throbbing,
the flame leaped and the smoke climbed
and surged every way:
blinding of eyes, splitting of hearing.

And after it, the six men dead
the whole day;
among the shells snoring
in the morning,
and again at midday
and in the evening.

In the sun, which was so indifferent,
so white and painful;
on the sand which was so comfortable,
easy and kindly;
and under the stars of Africa,
jewelled and beautiful.

Ghabh aon Taghadh iadsan
's cha d' ghabh e mise,
gun fhaighneachd dhinn
cò b' fheàrr no bu mhiosa:
ar leam, cho diabhlaidh coma
ris na sligean.

Sianar marbh rim o ghualainn
latha foghair.

SOMHAIRLE MacGILL-EAIN

One Election took them
and did not take me,
without asking us
which was better or worse:
it seemed as devilishly indifferent
as the shells.

Six men dead at my shoulder
on an Autumn Day.

SORLEY MacLEAN

Green Boughs

My young, dear friends are dead,
All my own generation.
Pity a youthless nation,
Pity the girls unwed,
Whose young lovers are dead.
They came from the gates of birth
To boyhood happy and strong,
To a youth of glorious days,
We give them honour and song,
And theirs, theirs is the praise.
But the old inherit the earth.
They knew what was right and wrong,
They were idealists,
Clean minds, my friends, my friends!
Artists and scientists,
Their lives that should have been long!
But everything lovely ends.
They came from college and school,
They did not falter or tire,
But the old, the stupid had rule
Over that eager nation,
And all my own generation
They have cast into the fire.

NAOMI MITCHISON

The Mother

'Mother, o' mine; O Mother o' mine.'

My mother rose from her grave last night,
  And bent above my bed,
And laid a warm kiss on my lips,
  A cool hand on my head;
And, 'Come to me, and come to me,
  My bonnie boy,' she said.

***

And when they found him at the dawn,
  His brow with blood defiled,
And gently laid him in the earth,
  They wondered that he smiled.

JOSEPH LEE

The Permanence of the Young Man

No man outlives the grief of war
Though he outlive its wreck:
Upon the memory a scar
Through all his years will ache.

Hopes will revive when horrors cease;
And dreaming dread be stilled;
But there shall dwell within his peace
A sadness unannulled.

Upon his world shall hang a sign
Which summer cannot hide:
The permanence of the young men
Who are not by his side.

WILLIAM SOUTAR

Final Poems & What They Mean to Me

There are many poems that we forget. There are others that we may remember, as well as being able to bring to mind the exact circumstances of our first encounter with the poem in question. I remember very vividly the first time I read Robert Burns' 'A Man's a Man for A' That'. I was fourteen, and the poem made me cry. It was embarrassing, because we read the poem at school, in a class of tough boys, and none of the others cried. No poem had ever done that to me before (and I read a lot of poetry when I was young, much of it anthologised in Arthur Mee's *Children's Encyclopaedia*, an extraordinary twenty-volume encyclopaedia over which I poured for long hours from the age of nine onwards.) This poem is one of the greatest and most inspiring statements of the values that we think Scotland embraces. It is about something very deep the way Scotland sees herself when she looks in the mirror.

A Man's a Man for A' That

Is there for honesty poverty
That hings his head, an' a' that;
The coward slave – we pass him by,
We dare be poor for a' that!
For a' that, an' a' that,
Our toils obscure an' a' that,
The rank is but the guinea's stamp,
The man's the gowd for a' that.

What though on hamely fare we dine,
Wear hoddin grey, an' a' that?
Gie fools their silks, and knaves their wine,

A man's a man for a' that.
For a' that, an' a' that,
Their tinsel show, an' a' that,
The honest man, tho' e'er sae poor,
Is king o' men for a' that.

Ye see yon birkie ca'd a lord,
Wha struts, an' stares, an' a' that;
Tho' hundreds worship at his word,
He's but a coof for a' that.
For a' that, an' a' that,
His ribband, star, an' a' that,
The man o' independent mind
He looks an' laughs at a' that.

A price can mak a belted knight,
A marquise, duke, an' a' that;
But an honest man's aboon his might,
Gude faith, he maunna fa' that!
For a' that, an' a' that,
Their dignities an' a' that,
The pith o' sense, an' pride o' worth,
Are higher rank than a' that.

Then let us pray that come it may,
(As come it will for a' that,)
That Sense and Worth, o'er a' the earth,

Shall bear the gree, an' a' that.
For a' that, an' a' that,
That man to man, the world o'er,
Shall brithers be for a' that.

ROBERT BURNS

Burns acknowledged his debt to Robert Fergusson, the young poet whose life came to a sad end in Edinburgh's Bedlam hospital. Burns sought out his grave in the Canongate Kirkyard and found no stone. He remedied this. Today there is a statue just outside the kirk, a very popular representation of Fergusson, striding jauntily down towards Holyrood. In our own times, Robert Garioch attended a gathering of Fergusons in the kirkyard, there to honour the poet's memory. The sonnet he composed is immensely powerful. Here, he reminds us, Robert Burns himself knelt and kissed the grave-soil.

At Robert Fergusson's Grave

October 1962

Canongait Kirkyaird in the failing year
is auld and grey, the wee rosiers are bare,   *rose bushes*
five gulls leam white agin the dirty air: *gleam*
why are they here? There's naething for them here.

Why are we here oursels? We gaither near
the grave. Fergusons mainly, quite a fair
turn-out, respectfu, ill at ease, we stare
at daith – there's an address – I canna hear.

Aweill, we staund bareheidit in the haar,   *oh well; mist*
murnin a man that gaid back til the pool   *went back to the pool*
twa-hunner year afore our time. The glaur   *mud*

that haps his banes glowres back. Strang,   *covers his bones*
      present dool   *sorrow*
ruggs at my hairt. Lichtlie this gin ye daur: *disparage this if you dare*
here Robert Burns knelt and kissed the mool.   *earth (on a grave)*

ROBERT GARIOCH

Here is another example of one poet reflecting on the fate of another. Douglas Young, the St Andrews classicist and poet, reflects here on Willie Soutar, whose life was so constrained by illness but who, in a time of tyrants, testified truth. That was the 1930s, but perhaps we should not be complacent . . .

This moving tribute to Soutar was published in Young's *A Braird o Thristles*. I find the lines of the poem, particularly accompanied by George Bain's striking Celtic illustrations, extremely moving.

For Willie Soutar

Twenty year beddit, and nou
  the mort-claith.
This suld gar ilk ane grue,
  sic a daith.

Was his life warth livan? Ay,
  siccar it was.
He was eident, he was blye
  in Scotland's cause.

Liggan quate, his hairns were thrang
  for libertie,
his pen wove thegither sang
  and musardrie.

In the time of tyrants he
  testified truth,
and sae our yirth bydes aye free,
  saut wi fresh youth.

Sic smeddum, kindliness, and wit,
  hop and faith,
   nour that his corp is by wi it,
    outlive daith.

DOUGLAS YOUNG

Ruthven Todd was another poet who was a young man during those difficult years of the nineteen-thirties. His poem 'In September 1937' evokes the feeling of crisis of that time. He remembers being on Mull in another year altogether, and that takes him back to the island where the hills 'were brown lions, crouched to meet the autumn gales'. In the final verse, crisis is forgotten in the pleasure of sitting before the fire conversing with friends. Even so, this is one of the saddest – and most beautiful – poems I know.

In September 1937

Coming, in September, through the thin streets,
I thought back to another year I knew,
Autumn, lifting potatoes and stacking peats
On Mull, while the Atlantic's murky blue
Swung sluggishly in past Jura, and the hills
Were brown lions, crouched to meet the autumn gales.

In the hard rain and the rip of thunder,
I remembered the haze coming in from the sea
And the clatter of Gaelic voices by the breakwater,
Or in the fields as the reapers took their tea;
I remembered the cast foal lying where it died,
Which we buried, one evening, above high-tide;

And the three rams that smashed the fank-gate,
Running loose for five days on the moor
Before we could catch them – far too late

To prevent an early lambing the next year.
But these seemed out of place beside the chip-shop
And the cockney voices grumbling in the pub.

In September, I saw the drab newsposters
Telling of wars, in Spain and in the East,
And wished I'd stayed on Mull, their gestures
Frightened me and made me feel the unwanted guest,
The burden on the house who having taken salt
Could never be ejected, however grave his fault.

In September, we lit the fire and talked together,
Discussing the trivialities of a spent day
And what we would eat. I forgot the weather
And the dull streets and the sun on Islay,
And all my fear. I lost my count
Of the ticks to death, and was content.

RUTHVEN TODD

Muriel Spark was born one hundred years ago. She was an accomplished novelist and, in every sense, a surprising one. This poem, 'Going up to Sotheby's has all the hallmarks of her highly individual novels. It is very odd, which is what she succeeded so brilliantly at being.

Going Up To Sotheby's

This was the wine. It stained the top of the page
when she knocked over the glass accidentally. A pity, she said,
to lose that drop. For the wine was a treat.
Here's a coffee-cup ring, and another. He preferred coffee to
    tea.
Some pages re-written entirely, scored through, cancelled over
    and over
on this, his most important manuscript.

That winter they took a croft in Perthshire,
living on oats and rabbits bought for a few pence from the
    madman.
The children thrived, and she got them to school daily, mostly
    by trudge.
He was glad to get the children out of the way, but always
    felt cold
while working on his book. This
is his most important manuscript, completed 1929.
'Children, go and play outside. Your father's trying to work.
But keep away from the madman's house.'
He looked up from his book. 'There's nothing
wrong with the madman.' Which was true.

She typed out the chapters in the afternoons. He looked
      happily at her.
He worked best late at night.
'Aren't you ever coming to bed? I often wonder,
are you married to me or to your bloody book?'
A smudge on the page, still sticky after all these years.
Something greasy on the last page.
This is that manuscript, finished in the late spring,
crossed-out, dog-eared; this, the original,
passed through several literary hands while
the pages she had typed were at the publishers'.
One personage has marked a passage with red ink,
has written in the margin, 'Are you *sure*?'

Five publishers rejected it in spite of recommendations.
The sixth decided to risk his pounds sterling down the drain
for the sake of prestige. The author was a difficult customer.
      However,
they got the book published at last.
Her parents looked after the children while the couple went
      to France
for a short trip. This bundle of paper, the original manuscript,
went into a fibre trunk, got damp into it, got mouldy and furled.
It took fifteen more years for him to make his reputation,
by which time the children had grown up, Agnes as a
secretary at the BBC. Leo as a teacher.

The author died in '48, his wife in '68.
Agnes and Leo married and begat.
And now the grandchildren are selling the manuscript.
Bound and proud, documented and glossed
by scholars of the land, smoothed out
and precious, these leaves of paper
are going up to Sotheby's. The wine-stained,
stew-stained and mould-smelly papers are
going up to Sotheby's. They occupy the front seat
of the Renault, beside the driver.
They are a national event. They are going up
to make their fortune at last,
which once were so humble, tattered, and so truly working class.

MURIEL SPARK

The Clearances

The thistles climb the thatch. Forever
this sharp scale in our poems,
as also the waste music of the sea.

The stars shine over Sutherland
in a cold ceilidh of their own,
as, in the morning, the silver cane

cropped among corn. We will remember this.
Though hate is evil we cannot
but hope your courtier's heels in hell

are burning: that to hear
the thatch sizzling in tanged smoke
your hot ears slowly learn.

IAIN CRICHTON SMITH

Macpherson's Rant

Fare ye weel ye dark and lonely hills,
Far away beneath the sky.
Macpherson's time will not be long
On yonder gallows tree.

Sae rantinly, sae wantonly,
Sae dantinly gaed he.
He played a tune, an he danced it roon,
Ablow the gallows tree.

It was by a woman's treacherous hand
That I was condemned tae dee.
Upon a ledge at a window she stood
And a blanket she threw ower me.

The Laird o' Grant, that Hieland saunt,
That first laid hands on me.
He pleads the cause o' Peter Broon,
Tae let Macpherson dee.

Untie these bands frae off my hands
An' gie tae me my sword,
An' there's no a man in a' Scotland
But I'll brave him at a word.

For there's some come here tae see me hanged
An' some tae buy my fiddle
But before that I do part wi' her
I'll brak her through the middle.

He took the fiddle intae baith o' his hands
An' he brak it ower a stane.
Says no anither hand shall play on thee
When I am deid an' gane.

Farewell my ain dear Highland hame,
Fareweel my wife an' bairns.
There was nae repentance in my hert
When my fiddle was in my airms.

O, little did my mither think
When first she cradled me
That I would turn a rovin' boy
An' die on a gallows tree.

The reprieve was comin' ower the Brig o' Banff
Tae set Macpherson free.
Bit they pit the clock a quarter afore
An' they hanged him tae the tree.

ANON

The Flowers of the Forest

I've heard the lilting at our yowe-milking. *Singing*
  Lasses a-lilting before the dawn o' day;
But now they are moaning on ilka green loaning: *pasture*
  'The Flowers of the Forest are a' wede away.'

At buchts, in the morning, nae blythe lads are scorning; *sheepfolds*
  The lasses are lonely, and dowie, and wae:
Nae daffin', nae gabbin', but sighing and sabbing: *fooling around*
  Ilk ane lifts her leglen, and hies her away. *milkpail*

In hairst at the shearing, nae youths now are jeering,
  The bandsters are lyart, and runkled and grey; *grizzled*
At fair or at preaching, nae wooing, nae fleeching; *coaxing*
  The Flowers of the Forest are a' wede away.

At e'en in the gloaming, nae swankies are roaming
  'Bout stacks wi' the lasses at bogie to play,
But ilk ane sits drearie, lamenting her dearie:
  The Flowers of the Forest are a' wede away.

Dule and wae for the order sent out lads to the Border:
  The English, for ance, by guile wan the day:
The Flowers of the Forest, that foucht aye the foremost,
  The prime o' our land are cauld in the clay.

We'll hear nae mair lilting at our yowe-milking,
  Women and bairns are heartless and wae;
Sighing and moaning on ilka green loaning:
  'The Flowers of the Forest are a' wede away.'

JEAN ELLIOT

And we end with the hauntingly beautiful 'The Flowers of the Forest' by Jean Elliot. It relates the sorry tale of Flodden. Oh well. Much has happened in history – and in poetry. Did you hear the skirl of the pipes when reading it?

BIOGRAPHICAL NOTES

MARION ANGUS (1865–1946) was born in Sunderland,
the oldest daughter of the Rev. Henry Angus and his wife
Mary Jessie Watson, but moved back up to Scotland when
she was eleven. In Arbroath, Marion wrote colourful, witty
and perceptive diaries and articles. It was not until freed of
family responsibilities during the First World War that
she started to write poetry. Marion's work is modern and
imaginative in its approach. Her *Selected Poems* were published
by Polygon in 2006.

HAMISH BLAIR Little is know of Captain Hamish Blair
other than the fact that he was said to have been stationed at
Scapa Flow during the Second World War.

KATE Y.A. BONE (1897–1986) Kate Y.A. Bone was born in
Kirkcaldy. Her love of the Scots language developed from
family holidays in rural Fife. She attended the University of
Edinburgh and returned to Kirkcaldy to teach. Following her
marriage, in 1926, to William Bone, they moved to Colinton.
She wrote poetry without cessation from the age of twelve
when she won a literary competition. She wrote not to be
published, but for herself and her 'scribbler's itch'. Her only
published work was a pamphlet, *Thistle By-Blaws*, which was
published by Castlelaw Press in 1978.

GEORGE MACKAY BROWN (1921–1996) was born in Stromness, Orkney, which remained his lifelong inspiration. He studied in Edinburgh, where he met Edwin Muir. In 1941 he was diagnosed with tuberculosis and lived an increasingly reclusive life in Stromness. But in spite of his poor health he produced a stream of work from 1954 onwards, including the 1994 Booker Prize-shortlisted *Beside the Ocean of Time*. His *Collected Poems* (2006) was published by John Murray.

GEORGE BRUCE (1909–2002) was a radio and television arts producer and a poet. He co-produced the radio programmes *Scottish Art and Letters* and *Arts Review*. Later he was fellow in creative writing at Glasgow University (1971–73) and visiting professor in US and Australia. In 1975 and 1976 he was the executive editor of *The Scottish Review*, and in 1984 he was awarded an OBE. His book *Pursuit* won the Saltire Society Scottish Book of the Year award in 1999. His *Collected Poems* (2001) was published by Polygon.

GEORGE BUCHANAN (1506–1582) was born near Killearn in Stirlingshire. He was educated at the local grammar school, where he showed such aptitude that he was sent at the age of fourteen to the University of Paris. In 1537, James V recalled him to act as tutor to one of his sons, but his satirical writings led to his condemnation as a heretic and to his arrest and imprisonment for six years. On his release, despite his leanings towards Protestantism, he was made Classical tutor to the teenage Queen Mary.

ROBERT BURNS (1759–1796) was born in Alloway on 25 January, the oldest son of seven children. His family were poor farmers. By his mid-twenties, Burns was an accomplished writer of verse, and his first volume of poetry, *Poems, Chiefly in the Scottish Dialect*,was published to great acclaim in 1786. Burns' work shows irony, wit, romanticism and sentiment, as well as bawdy humour, a seemingly indiscriminate admiration for women, and a capacity for compassion and feeling for his fellow man.

WILLIAM DUNBAR (c.1460–c.1530) was born in East Lothian. He was closely associated with the 'Golden Age' of King James IV and its literature and produced a large body of which, after the Battle of Flodden, began to embrace spiritual subjects more often than secular ones.

JEAN ELIOT (1727–1805), also known as Jane Elliot, wrote one of the most famous versions of 'The Flowers of the Forest', a lament for the dead of the Battle of Flodden. Published in 1776, it is her only surviving work. Eliot's version has proved the most enduring.

ROBERT FERGUSSON (1750–1774) was born in Cap and Feather Close in Edinburgh. He anonymously published the first of a trio of pastorals, entitled 'Morning', 'Noon' and 'Night' (*Ruddiman's Weekly*). Fergusson subsequently enjoyed two years' patronage from *Ruddiman's*. Fergusson may have been afflicted by depression, and following a head injury he was admitted to Edinburgh's Bedlam madhouse where he died aged just twenty-four.

A new edition of his *Selected Poems* was published by Polygon in 2016.

ROBERT GARIOCH (1909–1981) Garioch's most well-known work is his satirical and humorous verse written in Scots. Garioch was also well-known as the translator into Scots of authors as disparate as Apolliniare, Pindar and the nineteenth-century Roman poet Guiseppe Belli. He was Writer-in-Residence at Edinburgh University and also worked as lexicographer and transcriber in the School of Scottish Studies, Edinburgh University. His poetry was published by Polygon in *Collected Poems* (2004).

W.S. GRAHAM (1918–1986) was born in Greenock. Graham trained as a structural engineer while studying literature and philosophy at night classes. He then studied at Newbattle Abbey, near Edinburgh. After 1943 he lived at Madron and Mevagissey in Cornwall, where poetry was his main employment. He published his first book in 1942 and his poems have been published in *New Collected Poems* (Faber, 2004).

SIR ALEXANDER GRAY (1882–1986) was in born in Lochee, Dundee. He was a civil servant and professor of Political Economy. Sir Alexander Gray's reputation abides not only in his own field but also as a Scots poet and the author of one of the most-quoted lines in modern Scottish poetry. He progressed through the universities of Edinburgh, Göttingen and Paris, started his career as a civil servant, and went on to hold a prominent position in the academic and public life of Scotland. He was made CBE in 1939 and knighted in 1947.

HAMISH HENDERSON (1919–2002) was born in Blairgowrie in Perthshire, was educated at Dulwich College and Cambridge University and served in North Africa and Italy with the 51st Highland Division during the Second World War. Along with his poetry, Hamish was well known as a songwriter, a translator and a pioneer in the field of Scottish folksong. A new edition of his collected poems is to be published by Polygon in 2019.

ROBERT HENRYSON (c.1420–c.1490) was born in Dunfermline but little else is known about his life, except that he was a schoolmaster. External evidence and the content of his poems suggest that he studied law in Glasgow and in Rome. His output was small, aside from his 'Testament of Cresseid' and the Fables, drawn from Aesop and the thirteenth-century Roman de Renart.

JAMES HOGG (1770–1835) was a Scottish poet, novelist and essayist. As a young man he worked as a shepherd and farmhand, and was largely self-educated. He was a friend of many of the great writers of his day, including Sir Walter Scott, of whom he later wrote an unauthorised biography. He became widely known as the Ettrick Shepherd, a nickname under which some of his works were published, and the character name he was given in the widely read series *Noctes Ambrosianae*, published in *Blackwood's Magazine*. He is best known today for his novel *The Private Memoirs and Confessions of a Justified Sinner*.

VIOLET JACOB (1863–1946) was born near Montrose and lived in India and England after marrying a British army officer, returning to Angus after her husband's death. She wrote fiction and poetry in English, but her best poetry was written in Scots, with a true ear for the dialect of her native country, pre-dating the upsurge of interest in Scots of the Scottish Renaissance with her collections *Songs of Angus* (1915) and *More Songs of Angus* (1918). Her only son was killed during the Battle of the Somme in 1916.

RODERICK WATSON KERR (1895–1960) was a journalist, poet and publisher. He served as a second Lieutenant in the Royal Tank Corps from 1916 and was awarded the MC for courage in action in 1918. His collection *War Daubs* was published in 1919, and though he continued to write poetry, his later work was in a more satirical vein. Kerr worked for the *Scotsman* and, for most of his life, the Liverpool *Daily Post*, and in the 1920s was one of the founders of *The Porpoise Press*, a small but influential Scottish literary publishing venture.

JOSEPH LEE (1876–1949) was a poet, journalist, artist and traveller whose poems and sketches gave the world a glimpse of life in the trenches and prison camps of the First World War. Almost forty, and an established journalist in 1914, Lee nevertheless joined the Black Watch, later taking a commission in the King's Royal Rifle Corps. He was captured and spent 1918 as a prisoner of war. His two books of war poetry, *Ballads of Battle* and *Work-a-Day Warriors* were published in 1916 and 1917 respectively. He wrote very little poetry after the war but pursued a successful career in journalism.

NORMAN MACCAIG (1910–1996) was born and educated in Edinburgh. He attended the Royal High School, studied Classics at the University and went on to train as a schoolteacher. When he retired from teaching he was appointed as Creative Writer in Residence at the University of Edinburgh and then joined the staff at the University of Stirling. MacCaig was awarded the Queen's Gold Medal for Poetry and many other distinctions. His *Collected Poems* was published by Polygon in 2005.

HUGH MACDIARMID (1892–1978) was born in Langholm. He trained to be a teacher, spent many years on and off as a journalist, served in the medical corps during the First World War, and founded the National Party of Scotland. A champion of the Scottish language for linguistic and political reasons, he spearheaded the Scottish Renaissance of the twentieth century and was, interestingly, a modernist and a communist. His book-length poem, *A Drunk Man Looks at the Thistle*, is considered to be one of the most important in twentieth-century literature.

ALBERT MACKIE (1904–1985), was born in Edinburgh. He was one of the first of the group of poets writing in revitalised Scots during the period that has come to be known as the Scottish Renaissance. He was a journalist, Scottish correspondent, editor of the *Edinburgh Evening Dispatch* and a poet. He was also the unofficial historian of the Heart of Midlothian football club, his study *The Hearts* was published in 1958.

SOMHAIRLE MacGILL-EAIN/SORLEY MacLEAN (1911–1996) was born on the island of Raasay. He studied in Edinburgh, fought in North Africa during the Second World War and taught in several schools, with a long spell as rector at Plockton High School. He was a highly influential figure at the heart of the Gaelic renaissance in Scotland and his work addressed great injustices, from the Highland Clearances to Rwanda, as well as love.

ELMA MITCHELL (1919–2000) Lanarkshire-born Elma Mitchell went south with a scholarship to Oxford and remained in England, working as a librarian for the BBC and latterly as a freelance writer and translator. Her compassionate insights into people's lives were collected in four books of poetry; *People Etcetera: Poems New and Selected* was published by Peterloo in 1987.

NAOMI MITCHISON (1897–1999) is best known as a novelist and for her role as a lifelong social commentator and political activist. During the war both her husband and brother were seriously wounded; she joined a Voluntary Aid Detachment at St Thomas's Hospital in London. Her early poetry was published in *The Laburnum Branch* in 1926.

EDWIN MORGAN (1920–2010), born in Glasgow, lived there all his life, except for service with the RAMC. Although his poetry is grounded in the city, the title of his 1973 collection, *From Glasgow to Saturn*, suggests the enormous range of Morgan's subject matter. He was Glasgow's first Poet Laureate (1999–2002), and the first to hold the post of 'Scots

Makar', created by the Scottish Executive in 2004 to recognise the achievement of Scottish poets throughout the centuries.

EDWIN MUIR (1887–1959) was born in Orkney but moved to Glasgow when he was fourteen. His poetic vision is strongly influenced by a longing for lost Edens and lost childhood, as well as by his apocalyptic sense of war and its aftermath. An influential critic as well as poet, he published seven volumes of poetry, collected most recently by Faber in 1984.

KATHLEEN RAINE (1908–2003) was half Scottish; the landscape of the Highlands and that of her childhood Northumbria find a place in her poetry, which largely explores the relationship between and man and nature. She was a scholar and critic and the founder of the *Temenos* review and the Temenos Academy.

TESSA RANSFORD (1938–2015) was born in Mumbai where her father was Master of the Mint. The family moved back to Britain in 1948. Dorothy McMillan asserted in the *Scottish Review of Books* that 'No one has done more for the cause of poetry in Scotland than Tessa,' and indeed it is hard to imagine what contemporary poetry in Scotland would be like without the Scottish Poetry Library, the School of Poets, the Callum Macdonald Poetry Pamphlet Memorial Award and a host of other projects, all initiated and nurtured by Ransford.

ALASTAIR REID (1926–2014) was a poet, essayist, traveller and a consummate translator, instrumental in bringing the poems of Neruda and Borges into English. He worked for over forty years as a foreign correspondent for the *New Yorker*. *Inside Out: Selected Poetry and Translations* was published by Polygon in 2008.

SIR WALTER SCOTT (1771–1832) was born in Edinburgh. He studied law and moved to live in the Borders in 1799. There he completed his collection of the best Border ballads; a series of long narrative poems followed. Scott then turned to fiction. The success of his fiction was significant enough for him to undertake the building of his house, Abbotsford, near Melrose; however, this stretched beyond the books' earnings and when his publisher crashed in 1825 he heroically dedicated the last years of his life to working off the debt. Two of his long narrative poems, 'The Lady of the Lake' and 'The Lay of the Last Minstrel', were published recently by Birlinn.

NAN SHEPHERD (1893–1981) was born at East Peterculter and died in Aberdeen. Her first novel, *The Quarry Wood*, was published in 1928, with two more following in the 1930s. Hill-walking was Shepherd's great love; her single collection of poetry *In the Cairngorms* (1934) expresses an intensity of deep kinship with nature. Nan Shepherd's novels were re-published in the late 1980s. *In the Cairngorms* was recently re-published by Galileo Publishing (2014), with a foreword by Robert Macfarlane. She joined those Scottish writers already honoured in Edinburgh's Makars' Court when a stone dedicated to her was placed there in 2000. And in 2016 Nan Shepherd was chosen to feature on the new Royal Bank of Scotland five-pound note.

IAIN CRICHTON SMITH (1928–1998) was born on the island of Lewis and spent most of his life as a schoolteacher in Glasgow and Oban, receiving an OBE in 1980. In his fiction and poetry in both English and Gaelic he viewed Scotland's culture, small communities and religion with a keen eye. *New Collected Poems* was published by Carcanet in 2011.

SYDNEY GOODSIR SMITH (1915–1975) was born in Wellington, New Zealand of Scottish parents. Goodsir Smith went to live in Edinburgh at the age of twelve when his father was appointed to a Chair of Medicine at the University. By 1940, he was writing poetry in Scots. Much of his work features aspects of his adopted city, in the spirit of his literary forebear Robert Fergusson.

WILLIAM SOUTAR (1898–1943) was born in Perth and overcame his ill-health to write poetry in celebration of 'the generosity of life', and much verse in Scots for children. While at university Soutar had begun an acquaintance with Christopher Grieve (Hugh MacDiarmid), submitting poems for his *Northern Numbers*. Soutar became interested in the cultural renaissance MacDiarmid was promoting, though they did not entirely agree on the use of Scots; Soutar's own conviction was that rejuvenation of the language was necessary. After Soutar's death in 1943, collections of his poetry were edited by Hugh MacDiarmid (1948), and the librarian W.R. Aitken (1961 and 1988), but none is complete. Alexander Scott's 1958 biography of Soutar remains the only one.

MURIEL SPARK (1918–2006) was born in Edinburgh and lived most of her adult life in England and Italy. One of the most highly regarded British novelists of the twentieth century, notably as the author of *The Prime of Miss Jean Brodie*, she herself wrote 'I have always thought of myself as a poet.' She mischievously uses the poetic conventions while unsettling them, and her themes echo those of the novels, personal and metaphysical. Her collected poems are published by Carcanet.

ROBERT LOUIS STEVENSON (1850–1894) was born in Edinburgh. The ill health that dogged him from his earliest childhood provided him with the space and time in which his imagination could flourish; it also gave him the constant companionship of his nurse, who fed him a diet of Bible stories and Covenanting history, as well as tuning his young ear to a rich variety of the Scots language. Most famous for his novels, Stevenson was also a poet. He is probably best known for *A Child's Garden of Verses*, but he also wrote much lyric poetry, and a range of lively verse in Scots. It was in his poetry that Stevenson most effectively expressed the pain of his separation from Scotland.

RUTHVEN TODD (1914–1978) a Scottish-born poet, artist, novelist and early scholar of William Blake, was born in Edinburgh, where he was raised and educated, at Fettes College and Edinburgh College of Art. He spent most of his life outwith Scotland, in London, the USA and Spain. He was an artist, amateur botanist and novelist but is best known as a poet and writer of children's books.

MARY, QUEEN OF SCOTS (1542–1587), the only surviving legitimate child of King James V, was six days old when her father died and she acceded to the throne. In 1558 she married Francis, the Dauphin of France, but he died in 1561, shortly after his accession. That year she returned to Scotland and claimed the throne. She pursued a conciliatory religious policy, but her second marriage to her cousin Henry, Lord Darnley, his murder, and her subsequent marriage to the Earl of Bothwell outraged the nobility, who overthrew her in 1567 and imprisoned her in Lochleven Castle.

DOUGLAS YOUNG (1913–1973) was a poet and essayist. He studied at the Universities of St Andrews and Oxford and taught at the University of Aberdeen. He became a leading member of the young Scottish National Party and was imprisoned for refusing conscription in 1942, where he completed his first collection, *Auntran Blads*. He was a master of translation into Scots and had an international reputation as scholar of Greek, teaching classics in North America from the 1960s until his death.

ACKNOWLEDGEMENTS

We are grateful to the following publishers, authors and
estates who have generously given us permission to publish
these poems:

Marion Angus: 'Mary's Song' from *The Singin Lass: Selected Work
of Marion Angus* (Polygon, 2006) by permission of Polygon;
Kate Y.A. Bone: 'Some Ghaists Haunt Hooses' from *Thistle
By-Blaws* (Castlelaw Press, 1971) by permission of Reinold
Gayre, Minard Castle; George Mackay Brown: 'A New Child:
ECL', 'Beachcomber' and 'Hamnavoe' from *Collected Poems*
(John Murray, 2006) by permission of John Murray; George
Bruce: 'Departure and Departure and . . .', 'An Island and Seals',
'Boys among Rock Pools', 'Child on the Beach', 'Shetland and
Ponies', 'The Child and the Sea' and 'Voyage We to Islands'
from *Today Tomorrow: The Collected Poems of George Bruce
1933–2000* (Polygon, 2001) by permission of Polygon; Robert
Fergusson: 'from Auld Reekie' from *Selected Poems* (Polygon,
2007) by permission of Polygon; Robert Garioch: 'At Robert
Fergusson's Grave', 'Did You See Me', 'Glisk of the Great', 'In
Princes Street Gardens' from *Collected Poems* (Polygon, 2004)
by permission of Polygon; W.S. Graham: 'The Night City' from
Collected Poems (Faber, 1980). Reproduced by permission of
Rosalind Mudaliar, the estate of W.S. Graham; Sir Alexander
Gray: 'Scotland' from *Gossip: a book of new poems* (Porpoise

Press, 1928); 'On a Cat, Ageing' also form *Gossip: a book of new poems* (Porpoise Press, 1928); Hamish Henderson: 'So Long', 'Flyting O' Lif and Daith', 'Freedom Come All Ye' and 'The 51st Highland Division's Farewell to Sicily' from *Collected Poems and Songs* (Curly Snake Publishing, 2000) and 'Seventh Elegy: Seven Good Germans' from *Elegies from the Dead in Cyrenaica* (Polygon, 2008) published with permission of The Estate of Hamish Henderson; Roderick Watson Kerr: 'From the Line' from *War Daubs: Poems* (John Lane, 1919) by permission of Neil Kerr; Joseph Lee: 'The Mother' from *Ballads of Battle* (John Murray, 1916); Norman MacCaig: 'Basking Shark', 'Christmas Snow in Princes Street', 'Incident', 'Memorial', 'Toad' and 'True ways of knowing' from *Collected Poems* (Polygon, 2005) by permission of Polygon; Hugh MacDiarmid: ' "Scotland small?" ' from *Complete Poems, Vol. II* (Carcanet, 1994), 'At My Father's Grave' and 'Island Funeral' from *Collected Poems* (Carcanet, 2017) by permission of Carcanet; Albert Mackie: 'Molecatcher' from *Poems in Two Tongues* (The Darien Press, 1928); Somhairle MacGill-Eain / Sorley MacLean: 'Latha Foghairpoem / An Autumn Day', 'An Roghainn / The Choice', 'Curaidhean / Heroes', 'Hallaig', 'Latha Foghairpoem / An Autumn Day', 'Tràighean / Shores' from *A White Leaping Flame: Collected Poems* (Polygon, in association with Carcanet, 2011) by permission of Carcanet; Elma Mitchell: 'At First My Daughter' from *People Etcetera: Poems New and Selected* (Peterloo Poets, 1987) and 'Mother, Dear Mother' from *The Human Cage* (Peterloo Poets, 1979); Naomi Mitchison: 'Green Boughs' from *The Laburnum Branch* (Jonathan Cape, 1926); Edwin Morgan: 'King Billy', 'One Cigarette', 'Strawberries' and 'The Starlings in George Square' from *New Collected Poems* (Carcanet, 1992) by permission of Carcanet; Edwin Muir: 'Childhood', 'The Heart Could Never Speak', 'The Horses' and 'The Transmutation' from *Collected Poems* (Faber, 1984) by permission of Faber; Kathleen Raine: 'Invocation' from *Collected Poems* (Golgonooza Press, 2000); Tessa Ransford: 'Lily of Raasay' and 'Nocturne Lewis' from *Not Just Moonshine: New and Selected Poems* (Luath, 2008) by permission of Moray Stiven; Alastair Reid: 'Daedelus', 'Propinquity' and 'Scotland' from *Weathering: Poems and Translations* (Canongate, 1978) by permission of Canongate; Nan Shepherd: 'Loch Avon', 'Summit of Corrie Etchachan' and 'The Hill Burns' from *In the Cairngorms* (Galileo, 2015) by permission of Erland Clouston; Iain Crichton Smith: 'On Looking at the Dead', 'The Clearances' and 'The Shadows' from *New Collected Poems* (Carcanet, 2011) by permission of Carcanet; Sydney Goodsir Smith: 'For My Newborn Son' from *Collected Poems 1941–1975* (John Calder, 1975, 2010) by permission of Alma Books Ltd; William Soutar: 'The Permanence of the Young Man' from *Selected Poems of William Soutar* (Argyll Publishing, 2000), 'To the Future' from *Poems of William Soutar: A New Selection* (Scottish Academic Press, 1988), 'Winter's Awa' from *Seeds in the Wind: poems in Scots for children* (London: Andrew Dakers, 1943); Muriel Spark: 'Going Up To Sotheby's' from *All the Poems: Collected Poems* (Carcanet, 2004) by permission of Carcanet; Ruthven Todd: 'In September 1937', 'In Edinburgh 1940', 'Personal History' and 'Watching You Walk' from *Garland for the Winter Solstice* (Dent, 1961) by permission of Christopher Todd; Douglas Young: 'For Willie Soutar' from *Naething Dauntit: The Collected Poems of Douglas Young* (Humming Earth, 2016).

A NOTE ON THE TYPE

A Gathering is set in Verdigris MVB – a typeface designed by Mark van Bronkhorst. It is a Garalde text family for the digital age and is inspired by work of sixteenth-century punchcutters Robert Granjon, Hendrik van den Keere and Pierre Haultin.